Cosmic End-Time Secrets

by

Wallace C. Halsey

&

Alfred Steber

Containing the Collected Writings , Lectures and Charts of Dr. W. C. Halsey , the noted UFO researcher and teacher of NEW AGE truths. Dr. Halsey's scientific and Super - Sensory findings

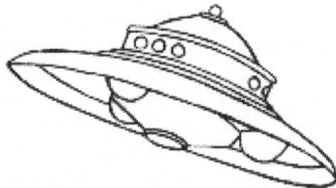

SAUCERIAN PUBLISHER
Original Sources in Ufology

ISBN: 978-1-955087-64-3

INTRODUCTION

CHAPTERS

INTRODUCTION

This book, "COSMIC END- TIME SECRETS", delivers back into your hands a large portion of your inheritance, a part of the Cosmic Light Treasure long hidden from you by negative forces on this planet .

It is my pleasure to introduce to you the amazing man whose life work culminated in this important book. His name is Dr. Wallace C. Halsey , D.D. , L. L.D. , professional engineer , scholar and minister.

Dr. Halsey's scientific background and education plus his personal experience in spiritual and New Age work, enabled him to speak on a wide range of topics . Not only did he lecture on the fascinating theme of " UFO's " (Unidentified Flying Objects) and their purpose, but also every other related subject you could possibly think of.

For instance, the Hollow Earth mystery. In this book you will read his full confidential report of his search in the far north region , for the Opening that leads into the interior of this world . Certainly it was tremendous adventure, and Dr. Halsey shares that adventure with you. He lectured also on the story of creation, the Tower of Babel, our solar system imbalance, functions of the Pyramids , the Infinite Light , squaring the body, the Pineal gland or "Third Eye " development, Teleportation , the work of the Melchizedek Order, Cosmic High Noon, the Transitor Beam, the White Stone, the Solar Tongue , and more.

Dr. Halsey was a cousin of the famous Fleet Admiral "Bull" Halsey , and served with him in the same waters in war time. When WW-2 ended , Dr. Halsey launched his own serious campaign to help anchor the principle of human brotherhood on earth, to take the place of conflicts . He knew how desperately earthlings need a higher level of LIFE , LOVE and LIGHT , and with the aid of his wife Tarna Halsey , and the "brothers upstairs " he served tirelessly . And in 1956 Dr. Halsey founded the Christ Brotherhood.

I first met Dr. Halsey in 1959. He was giving a talk in his home in Los Angeles . As I listened to him speak on one of the topics you will read about in this very book, I felt an immediate sense of kinship with him, as though we had known one another in some "pre- existent" state, long since lost to my conscious memory recall . In his presence I felt that "all things are possible " to the Inner Man. From my own all too brief personal contacts with Dr. Halsey , I can definitely tell you that he is (not was, but is) an unforgettable person.

riendly , affable , easy- going and generous -- YES ! But he was also powerfully magnetic, highly intuitive, persuasive and vibrant. I know of no one in New Age work who surpassed Dr. Halsey in fluency of speech , nor in the deep penetration of ideas. "These ideas, " he always reminded us, "are not just my own. This information is from OUT OF THIS WORLD, and it may seem very strange at first . But it is confirmed by your Holy Scriptures , by the 'Brothers Upstairs ' , and by science. "

His serious research in the field of Ufology led him to real contacts with beings not of this earth, and they unlocked many SECRETS for him and his loyal friends. The bulk of those secrets are contained in this book. Most of the chapters herein are taken from Tape -Recorded lectures given by Dr. Halsey , for he seldom wrote but lectured in many states including Alaska.

In 1962, as Dr. Halsey lay sleeping upon his bed, the "brothers upstairs " instructed Tarna to set up a taperecorder near his bed, turn it on and lay the microphone on his chest. She did so and, while still asleep , Dr. Halsey began to audibly channel the END- TIME message, and it is the same one that you will read in the final chapter of this book. Upon awaking later , and hearing the message on the tape, he expressed to Tarna his astonishment.

On March 27, 1963, while flying a light plane from Utah to Nevada, Dr. Halsey and his plane mysteriously disappeared and to this day have never been found. In my opinion he is now "upstairs " with the "brothers" and is in good hands. I am sure he is very pleased to know that a copy of his book reached you before the end-time deepens .

Herein are his Cosmic Secrets of the END- TIMES .

-- Michael X. Barton

Dr. Wallace C. Halsey , D.D. , L. L. D.

Noted UFO Researcher, electronic engineer, scholar of the scriptures, minister, author , founder of the Christ Brotherhood, Inc. , and dedicated exponent of unlimited, Cosmic truth.

> "FOR I WOULDST SPEAK TO THEE OF THE END-TIME, WHICH DRAWS NIGH -- AND OF THE STRANGE AND WONDROUS THINGS I SHALL CAUSE TO BEFALL THEE..."

CHAPTER 1
My Trip to the Great Door
◆

Recently a group of eight of us took a trip into the Arctic . We were looking for something . We were looking for the opening -- a Great Door -- leading into the INTERIOR of this world. This world is HOLLOW. Everything in creation is hollow. Even the hair of your head is hollow. And so we proceeded to go to Fairbanks , Alaska in the interior of Alaska , and after regrouping our forces and waiting for the heavy snows in the mountain passes near Eagle (north of Fairbanks) to clear, we continued Northward.

Part of our party followed the snowplows in, as far north as you can drive on the North American continent, up on the Yukon River to a little village named Circle , Alaska. My wife and I, and one of our party , followed four days later.

The thaw had really begun to show up and the blisters had begun to come up in the road until there were ruts 18-20 inches deep and went the width of the road, and sometimes 200 feet long . And we were trying to negotiate these ruts in a Cadillac automobile . So we would take a fast run -- maybe 60 or 65 miles an hour -- and hit them, and just glide over the top. Well , this worked for a few, until I broke an oil line underneath the car. So there I was stranded and I decided, well maybe this isn't such a good idea. If I can get someone to repair the automobile maybe we had better turn around and go back.

I set out on foot to see if I could find a sourdough cabin, or a miner or a trapper or someone who had transportation who could aid us. And the farther I walked the more I decided to give up the whole thing because of the condition of the road. Even for that time of year it was very serious . So I walked up over the road and guess what I saw? UFO's ! There were 5 of them sitting there, just as clear as anything you ever saw, at about 300 feet off of the surface of the road. There was no contact, but they sat there for a period of 2 minutes and then they were gone, just like that! Just like you'd turn an electric light off, they disappeared But we had the feeling in our consciousness that we were not alone. We had a feeling that this was a SIGNAL that we should go ahead. So we waited till a truck came, and I took a ride with the truck until I came to a " Jack of all trades" , a man who does trapping , runs a service station, does a little mechanical work, does a lot of exploring , does a little mining , and he has what they call a "Muskkeg Hopper" . It's an old military vehicle -- with airplane wheels on it that'll run over anything . And he came and got us, repaired the automobile, and in spite of the soft blemishes and everything in the road we proceeded on our way.

When we arrived at our destination in the north, we found that there was hardly anything at all , except some natives on the Yukon River and a few of these were employed on the river boats that operate during the summer months from the lower Yukon region to the Arctic of the far , far north, even up around Fort Yukon. There we had found that the University of Alaska had exploration teams going on even past Fort Yukon, and places in the far north up into the area of the Brooks Range in Alaska and north of the Brooks Range as far as they could travel . And there they took "Snow Caterpillars " or "Snow Trains " which are enclosed Caterpillar tractors for towing their food supplies and their work gear.

There they would go to an outpost, and from there they would take an airplane and fly up to a very secret camp in the north where they were said to be doing work for the organization that is the successor to the International Geophysical Year scientists. They said the nature of this is very SECRET . It is controlled by the Military . But they said that a certain amount of information had come through -- or leaked through --that reported they were very alarmed because a major base of exploration which our own Government had established , had recently been taken over by the Russian people and they were barring us from those entrances!

We asked about the feasibility and the opportunity to go across this area ourself and get as close to the opening into the interior of the world as we could. We'd like to even go INTO the interior. They said that, because of the international situation, and because of the way in which the military restrictions had been set up, it would be impossible to proceed to that location unless we had a clearance from the military and also we would have to have a helicopter . That was the only way we could negotiate that. But in spite of these obstacles, we were not discouraged.

We kept our eyes open, and we talked to people . One of those we talked with happened to be a bush pilot in this area. These are the boys who can fly without a compass or map to almost any part of Alaska . Questioning him regarding the site that we wanted to explore , as close by as we could, that is , we received a jolt . The pilot informed us that the location of the opening or "Doorway " into the interior of the world was closed -- even to our own government officials -- that the nation of the Soviet Union had taken it over, had just literally come over and set down and taken over that exploration site. Moreover, he said,

"On going into that area I have never failed to see, on flying in there, one or more flying saucers. " On the first occasion, I flew out of a cloud bank and right in front of me was a stationary , static object that was very round, shaped like a bell, and glowed very brightly . I thought it was going to run right into us, but as I got close it just raised up and I went right underneath and then it set down and I circled around and came back, and it just set there in the sky . So I looked it over real well . I didn't know what it was , but I thought that it must be what some folks call a "flying saucer" or unidentified flying object . Certainly it was unidentified as far as I was concerned.

"So I returned to Ladd Airforce Base at Fairbanks, Alaska and I told the briefing officers there (even though I was a civilian we have to make some type of report) that I had spotted a UFO , or what most people would call a flying saucer."

They said, "Military intelligence will want to talk to you . " They took him into an office , and wanted to know the size of the craft , the speed of the craft, whether it glowed with a greenish glow , reddish glow , or was white or colorless , and just what the composition was . They asked him if it looked metallic, or whether it looked like light . They wanted to know if it had openings you could call portholes , and if so, how many portholes ? They wanted to know all about this craft.

So the bush pilot gave a complete report that took an hour's time . When he had finished this , he thought that he'd be free to go, but they said, "Well now, wait a minute. You can't go just yet. We want to tell you that you did NOT see a flying saucer. " The pilot looked a trifle bewildered.

"But sir ,I did! And I just gave you a complete description and report!"

They said, "We repeat, you didn't see any UFO and you did not see a flying saucer. "After six hours in their offices, they said to him, "We know that you would like to go, but you did NOT see a UFO and you did NOT see a saucer."

He replied , "I have got things that I have to do. Time marches on! "

They persisted , "You did NOT see a flying saucer ! When will you get the point ?" He said, "I get the point ! I didn't see anything ! " "Then sign this paper here and we'll let you go.

So he said after this experience , if you get to talk to some of the other bush pilots that flew into this area they'll tell you "We have all gone thru this same experience one time. After that we become like little monkeys . We hear nothing , we see nothing and we say nothing . And that is the best way to keep out of the hair of the military . For some reason the boys up front want to keep this thing quiet, and for that reason we don't say anything about it."

I thought you would like to know some of these facts about the flying saucer story and why they don't get any farther than they do.

We found that it was quite impossible to go into this first area , but we remembered that George Van Tassel of Yucca Valley, California, about 3 years ago had published information that near a far north airforce base, there was an opening into the interior of the world. We knew quite well what airforce base it was close to, and you can guess which one easily . So we decided to look for that entrance.

So a group of us circled out through the wilderness around one side of this airforce installation on Government land, and we struck upon a road that was well travelled, but seemed to be more or less a restricted road. A sign said, "Government Property - Keep Out. " Have you ever seen those signs ? Well , here is the legal view we took of that sign . We took the same kind of view that Dr. Frank Stranges took when he was reporting the presence of a Venusian in the Pentagon for three years , one that he had conversed with. On bringing out the information about this Venusian, Dr. Stranges was confronted on several occasions by military intelligence that stated: "You must tell us what you are going to speak about so that we can censor it before you speak. "

Dr. Stranges cited the Constitution of the United States and they said, "Well sir , we represent the United States Government. " And he answered them by saying , "Yes , sir , I understand that, but sir , I - AM the United States Government! "

We remember that it's a Government of the people , by the people and for the people -- it says so in writing -- and we believe in keeping it that way, don't we ? So regarding this sign saying : "Government Property - Keep Out. " , we felt that anyone who was not a part of the Government should not go in there, you see?

So we proceeded down this road that belonged to us as far as we could go until we came to the Tanana River . This River parallels the road at the point where we had gone as far as we could go. The reason I say it was as far as we could go was because we were getting a little too close. We were getting into a position where the military did not tell you to get out it was a position where if you took one more step you were "checked out" of the Government -- you know, by a BULLET . They'd check you OUT.

We saw a sign which I thought was most comprehensive and yet somewhat stupid , because it said:

"WARNING - GOVERNMENT PROPERTY . NO TRESPASSING . KEEP OUT . THERE IS NO REASON WHATSOEVER WHY YOU SHOULD PROCEED BEYOND THIS POINT. "

And then down below this statement was written , " NO, NUTHIN! " Beyond this was the wire and you step over that and then the military will take the toll of YOU . So we knew from the position that we were in, that we were on the very surface of the property of the OPENING into the interior of this world , but if we'd taken another step we'd have lost our lives .

However , we were able to glean a lot of information from the Indians. The Indians have a tradition. They pass things down from one to another. They stated that their origin was from out of the north. We asked, " How far north?" They said, "You don't understand... from OUT of the north. " And they drew a circle as it were, indicating a great hole or opening into this world, and they repeated , "Our origin is OUT of the north. We came OUT of the north. " Their lore includes the idea of a HOLLOW EARTH.

We are told that the time is coming when there is going to be a GREAT TRIBULATION on the surface of this world . But there is another side to the coin, as it were. For we are also told of a GLORIOUS time. In Isaiah 13 it says, "I heard songs, singing glory to the Father" , and about that time we were all gathered in the CLEFT of a rock.

Now you show me the cleft of a rock that is large enough to take care of all of us. I mean ALL of us. Did you ever stop to think WHERE the cleft of the rock might be ? Some say it is in the Rock, Christ Jesus . It sure is ! But it is also in a physical place ! Because remember , that we're going to be glorifying the Lord , Yahveh, out of the fire . We're going to stand in those fires ! We are going to stand boldly right in the fire.

If you are going to be of the Son of Man -- which means those who sow the seed in the good ground -- then you are going to be on the front . And you're going to be in a position to glorify the Lord , out of the fires , because believe me, you'll be standing right in the middle of them. But the Master said, "I will quicken you in your mortal body. " He didn't say, "I will quicken your mortal body" , but "I will quicken YOU in your mortal body. " This spiritual quickening will cause you to feel the hand come inside of your hand , and a hand come in the other side in the other hand. And a foot will grow inside of each foot, for He said, "I'll walk in you and I'll talk in you, and I'll be the Head of the family . I'll be the Lord YAHVEH to you and you'll be My Son.

And then, no man will be able to stand before you. Then you can face an army . Then a hook will be put under your jaw and you'll be TURNED around. Because, without you, there'll be no hook put in any jaw . Because you are the ones that are chosen to stand forth in the END- TIMES.

Listen. I don't care what your PHYSICAL age is. According to Genesis II , chapter 1, we're all the same age. We're not looking only on the outer man, because the outer man certainly does deteriorate. However , the INNER man is renewed day by day . And that inner man is a very important person, because it is the Christ within you. And that is your hope of glory . This "glory " is the Intelligence of the Father Himself in you.

When that GLORY begins to shine forth -- that very Intelligence -- it says that no man will be able to stand before you.

Why would there be a place in the far Arctic North to which a group of people -- not only this group but other groups -- are being sent ? Let me tell you what we ran across . You know we Ministers, wherever we are, if we see someone who is crooked, we'll straighten them. To give you an example , coming back on the airplane from Alaska, I started to talk to the stewardess. There was one seat available in the airplane and it was next to me. And she sat down for "take - off" and fastened her seat- belt . I started a conversation. And the first thing you know, I was telling her about some of these things. She expressed a very deep interest.

She's on our mailing list now, because on the airplane we had a "NewAge" lecture of 5-1/ 2 hours duration, from Anchorage , Alaska to Seattle!

We talked to a group this last week in Fairbanks. A lady came to the place where we were staying , and she said: "I've heard things that you have been saying through a newsletter that a friend of mine sent to me, and I saw your name mentioned. Could you be the same person? "Well, " I said, "I guess I could. " So she just took her gloves off and sat down. She said, "All right , start talking!"

I noticed that she had a brace on her right leg , like she had suffered polio or something . It turned out that she had been in a terrible accident and had to have a bone graft . Well , we talked for a while and I thought , "That's probably all she can chew, " But she said, "Oh no, tell me more!" So we came to the part about the healing power of the All - Father, and one of the group there said , "I'd like to see that brace come off -- the doctors say not to dare walk without it. " I said, speaking to the crippled woman, "We'll see how you feel. Stand up. " She stood up and we prayed for her.

She didn't take the brace off right then, but she said, "I feel the strangest things like ELECTRICITY is going all through my body and my leg is hot! " The next day she was seen walking briskly down the street without her brace. She is the corresponding secretary for the Chamber of Commerce in Fairbanks, Alaska.

The word spread . Pretty soon a couple contacted us and said, " Doctor, I don't know how to explain this , really , do you ? But we've been praying for about 4 or 5 years that someone would come and bring us truth. We are so isolated here we do not get the information that you would give in California or some of the other places . However , we did receive a message from the Father in which He said: 'Build a place . Build a place for meeting and I'll send somebody . ' So about a week ago, we finished this place ." "What kind of a place ?" I asked.

"A place for meetings . We have a little group formed here, for study of spiritual things . Anything that we can study to get some truth is welcome. Would you come over and talk to us? "

"Sure ! I'll go over and talk. " Suddenly another person spoke up and said, "Well, you can't possibly get there before 9 O'clock, because I want you to talk before a group of business men at the Chamber of Commerce building first . They're having a dinner tonight and I want you to talk to them. " And I said, "All right."

So I went to talk to the group of business men. After that we went out to this other place of meeting and I expected to see maybe a Quonset hut or something thrown together crudely , you know, for a meeting place ? Here was a building that cost about $65,000.00 dollars . And it was dedicated to a better life in the New- Age understanding . Well, I was so imbued with the spirit of their own courage and devotion I talked to them until one O'clock in the morning . "Don't stop! " they said.

"I'm going to have to stop, " I replied , "but I'll come back. Yes , I'll come back, and there will be others that will come. Because I believe that the way the Plan is being formed, is that where we are going there is going to be a new road built, across the North, by footsteps . And maybe we'll even have a little extra help from the " boys upstairs " to where we won't have to use so many footsteps . But we're looking now, for an OPENING into the interior of the cleft in the rock . And we intend to find it and it is not going to be easy. It is tough traveling . But the Father says, "I will have my strong ones on the front line. " And let me tell you , you are going to have a surprise . Because when you get there to the front line there is going to be far more POWER than you've enjoyed here.

There's kind of a little game going with a few of us in Fairbanks . We have felt the charged power of the INFINITE LIGHT of the Father in that place so strong it is truly an electrifying experience . If we would, say, go into a restaurant there for some orange juice , or a glass of milk or a sandwich, people would FEEL this charge .

I know one restaurant man who will not make change for me unless he lays it down. "Because, " he says, "I can't touch you -- you knock me down! " He is a Greek. The same way with my wife and some of the others in our little group. The charge -force is so great the average person dare not come into direct contact, physically , with us. And believe me, this POWER is something that is within. It is not that which is without.

This world still holds many SECRETS that most people haven't even begun to suspect as yet. Many of these deeper secrets have to be revealed from within rather than by outer exploration alone, or by instruments. In the END- TIME of the Age -- right now -- the Father is revealing many wonderful things to all who will listen humbly , and act purposefully .

An article entitled : "Our Navy Explores Antarctica" , written by Rear Admiral Richard E. Byrd , in the October 1947 issue of The National Geographic Magazine plainly shows photographs of some of the South Pole area which happens to be TROPICAL . Where you would expect to find ice -fields and frozen wasteland, they have found ICE - FREE LAND. This "strange oasis" covers an area of 300 square miles. It was the most surprising discovery of the expedition . Surprising too, is the fact that almost everything in creation is HOLLOW, including our pear-shaped earth.

If it is hollow, logically there could be a DOOR which leads inside. We even went to look for the nearest entrance, and we got up to one near a far North Airforce Base that George Van Tassel told about, and if we'd felt like being tested out for bullets , we'd probably have taken one or two more steps. But I'll tell you, that one of these times , we expect to go into the INTERIOR of the world . WE REALLY EXPECT TO.

I might also tell you that Navy divers have gone down onto the floor of the Arctic ocean and they found a growth of vegetation that goes right on down into the INTERIOR of the world. At the Newsreel Theatre in downtown Los Angeles they showed a picture of this vegetation on the bottom of the Arctic ocean, and where it is going right on down into a big OPENING .

CHART 1
DR. HALSEY'S COSMIC CHARTS
INFINITE LIGHT

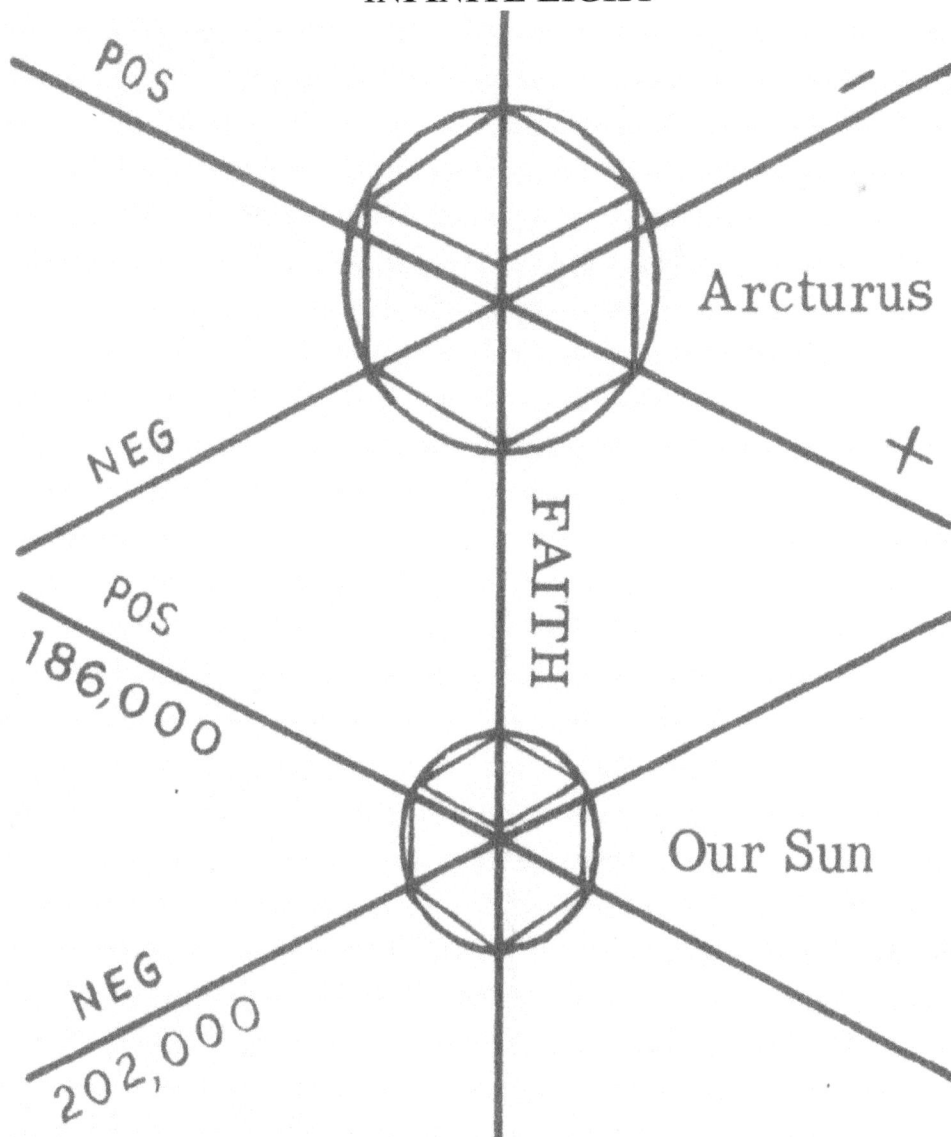

POS

−

Arcturus

NEG

+

FAITH

POS

186,000

Our Sun

NEG

202,000

TREE OF LIFE
(Explanatory text for Chart 2 is on pages 16, 17.) Chart 1 is on page 16.)

CHART 2
DR. HALSEY'S COSMIC CHARTS
INFINITE LIGHT

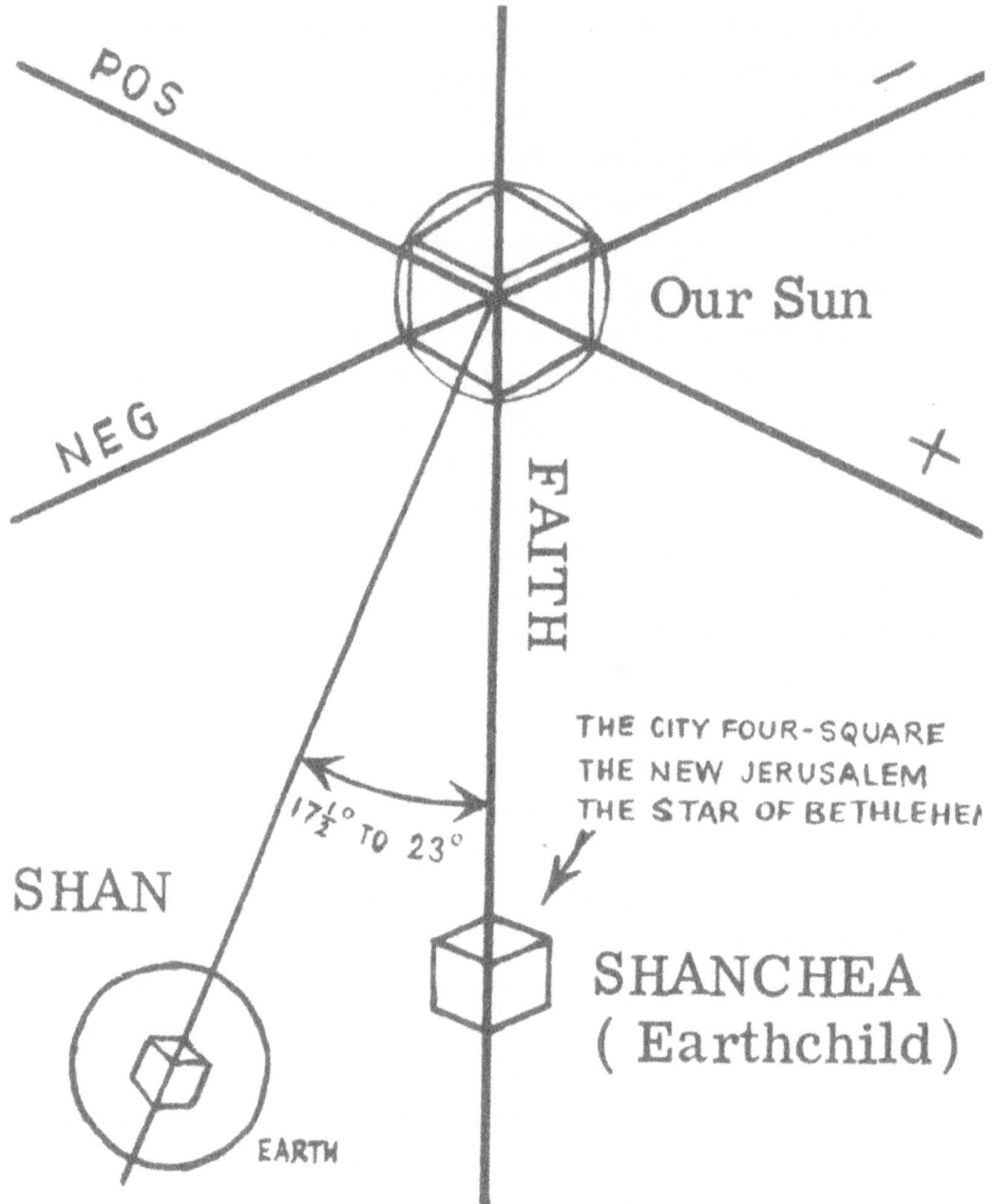

POS

—

Our Sun

NEG

+

FAITH

THE CITY FOUR-SQUARE
THE NEW JERUSALEM
THE STAR OF BETHLEHEM

$17\frac{1}{2}°$ TO 23°

SHAN

SHANCHEA
(Earthchild)

EARTH

EARTH OFF COURSE
(Explanatory text for Chart 2 is on page 18)

CHART 3

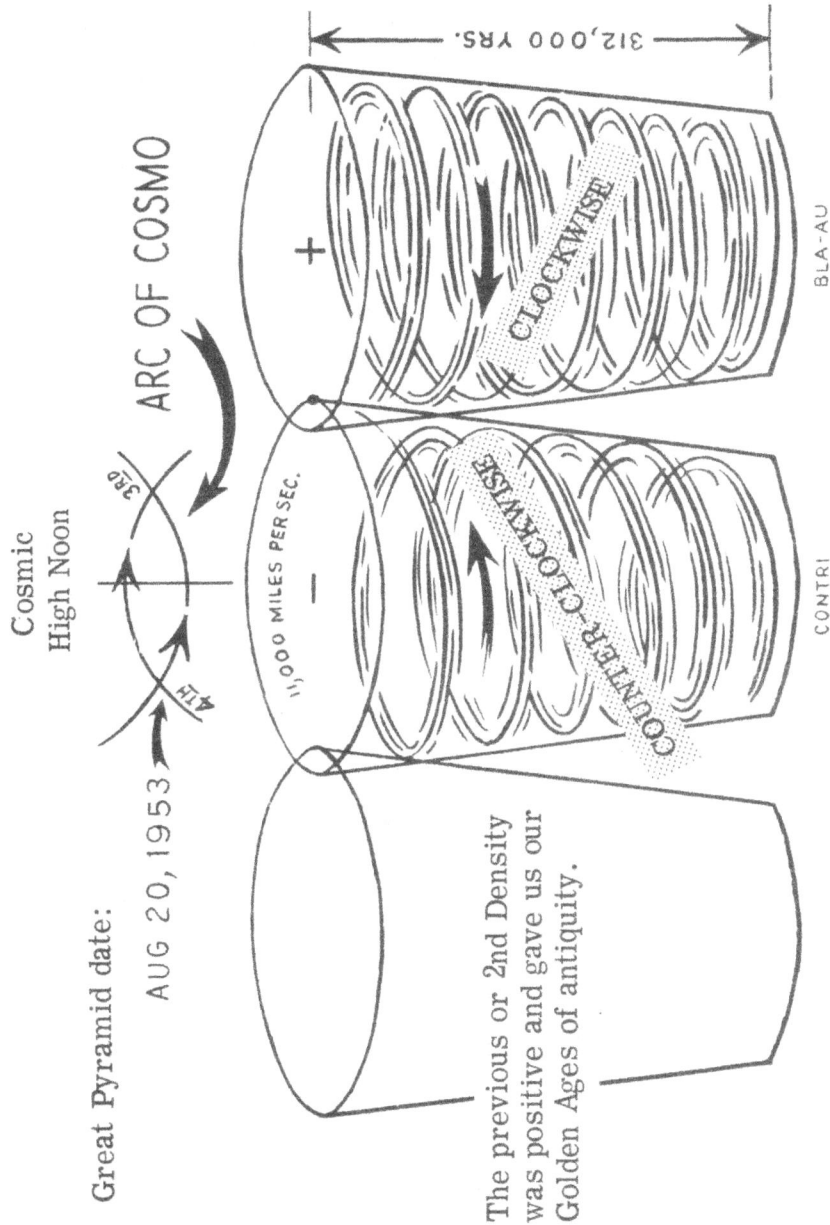

Cosmic High Noon

Great Pyramid date: AUG 20, 1953

ARC OF COSMO

4TH

3RD

11,000 MILES PER SEC.

CLOCKWISE

COUNTER-CLOCKWISE

312,000 YRS.

+

−

BLA-AU

CONTRI

The previous or 2nd Density was positive and gave us our Golden Ages of antiquity.

The 3rd Density is negative in polarity, oriented to matter.

The 4th Density is positive in polarity, oriented to mind.

Note: Refer to page 41

THIS COSMIC CHART SHOWS WHERE WE HAVE BEEN, WHERE WE ARE NOW, AND WHERE WE ARE GOING IN THE UNIVERSE. IT EXPLAINS THE "NEW AGE" AS BEING A POLARITY CHANGE.
(For Chart 3 see page 92)

CHART 4

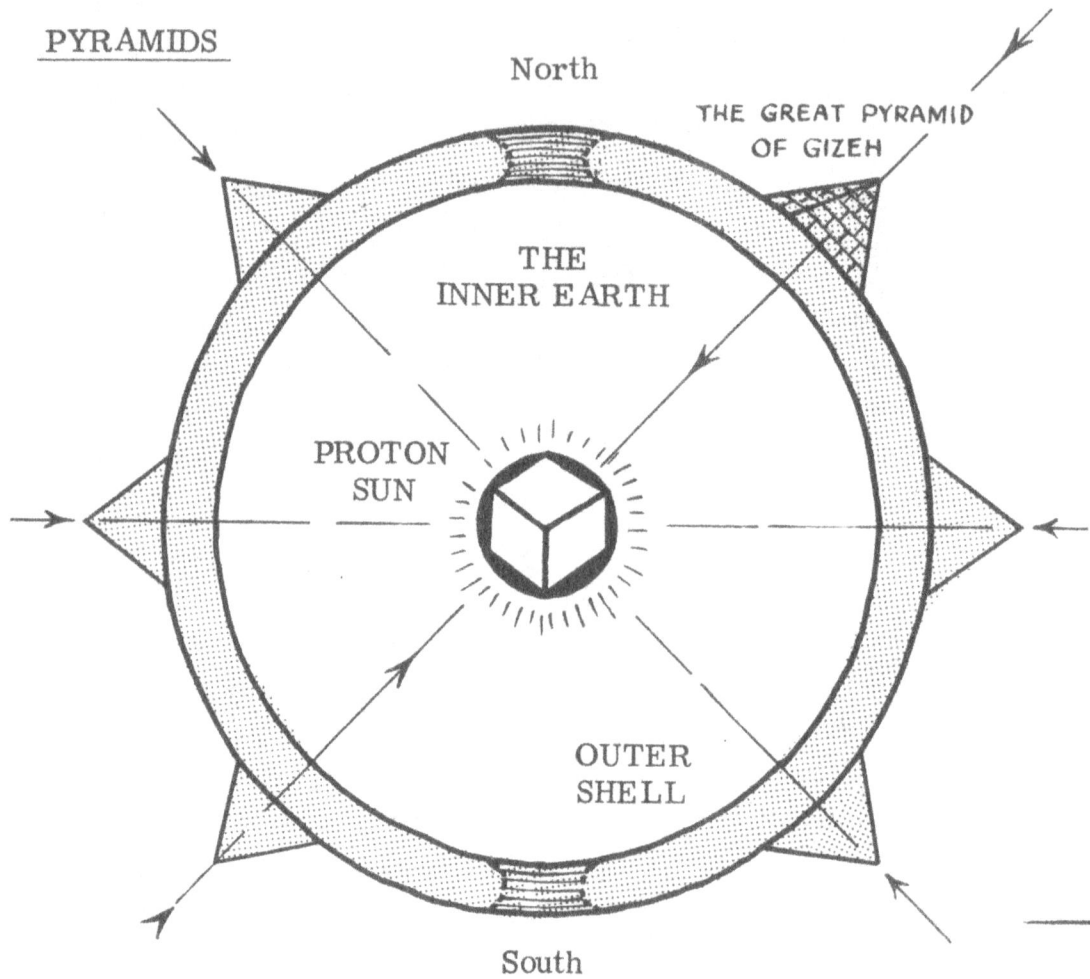

PYRAMIDS

North

THE GREAT PYRAMID
OF GIZEH

THE
INNER EARTH

PROTON
SUN

OUTER
SHELL

South

(Refer to pages 20-21 when studying this chart)

13

CHART 5

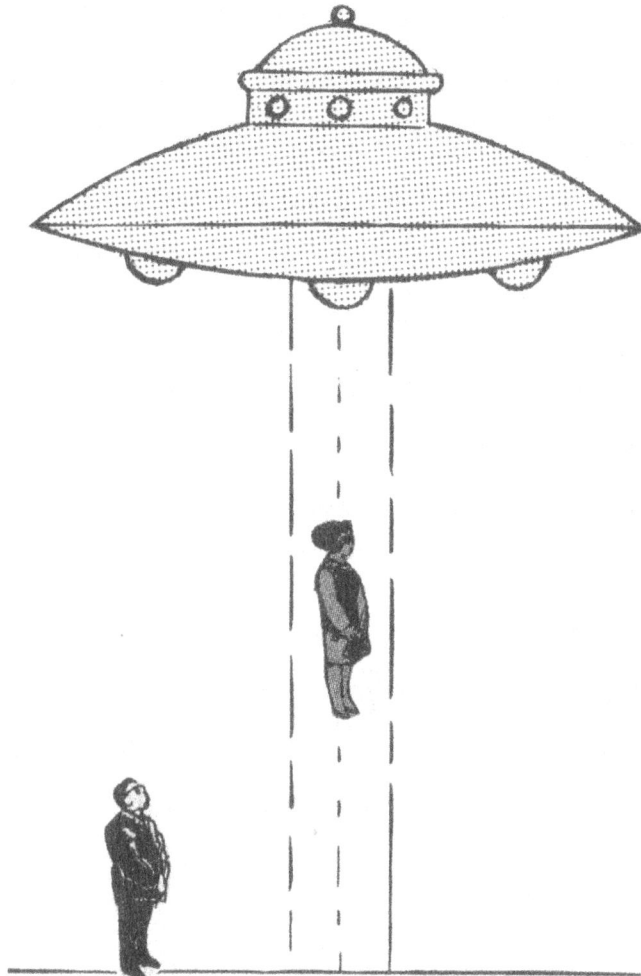

THE TRANSITION BEAM

(Read pages 88-89)

CHAPTER 2
Secrets of Infinite Light
◆

I'd like to ask you folks a question. How many of you have seen FIREBALLS .-- green fireballs -- go through the sky at one time or another ? My mother is here tonight -- would you raise your hand, mother? Thank you! I have an aunt which is my mother's sister . I want to tell you about her. She is just a kid -- 82 years old. She dresses like a kid, and certainly she doesn't act like she's eighty -two years old. But she's the type of person that was brought up with the Carrie Nation crowd -- remember the old WCTU[1] ?

She was a strict Methodist and strict about one thing and another. Well , she abr got to feeling pretty bad here some time ago, and she has a little heart condition. And the doctor said, "If you get a virus , it's liable to be the end of you! "

Well , she started to come down with a virus , and knowing of this heart condition, she was real worried. So our children had been visiting her. They and my aunt and my mother were standing on the front porch of the house in Los Angeles , California. My aunt just kind of looked up and said, " I always hear that the Space People from other planets are doing everything for everybody , but they won't do anything for me. I don't know why they can't do something for me if they can do something for everybody else. "

At about that time, the whole neighborhood lit up because a green FIREBALL came right through the sky and hit the corner of the house next door, and splattered just like it had been a tomato or something . Only it was green, and it was LIGHT . The next one HIT HER RIGHT IN THE CHEST and knocked her down. And she was hit by the third one, isn't that true ? And she was INSTANTLY HEALED of the virus infection. It was all taken away. So she has a deeper appreciation of the Brothers Upstairs , now.

It hasn't been too long ago, we were instructed by the "ones upstairs " to go to Washington . We didn't know why . We found out later it was to see one person,

---
1.Women's Christian - 14 - Temperance Union.

just one person. That person had an exact need that we were able to help , and administer to. Coming back to Los Angeles , my wife Tarna, had a fever of about 105 degrees . She had that old "Asiatic Flu".

We drove into Los Angeles during the middle of the night , and we thought we'd settle down and get her into bed where she should be. I think that when anyone has a 104-105 degree temperature they ought to be in bed, don't you ? But instead, we got instructed from upstairs to go to the desert to our little ranch out of Pioneertown. So we jumped in the automobile and went to Pioneertown and we couldn't figure out WHY .

When we got there we stood out under the stars on a moonlight night , full moon was just as bright as it could be. We didn't see a thing -- nothing extraordinary -- and it was almost daylight with the bright moonlight . I turned and put my arm around her and said, "Well , come on, we're going to take you in and put you to bed. " But before I could move, a CIRCLE OF LIGHT about 20 feet long , struck us both for as long as it takes to snap your finger , and I said, "What in the world was THAT ?" She said, "Honey, I've got no fever . I feel wonderful !" I put my hand on her head. Her forehead was perfectly cool. And we never did get to sleep . We never did get to sleep ! We went out looking to see where it had come from. Of course we realized we had been "beamed" from "upstairs "!

This evening, in "Secrets of Infinite Light " , we're going to take you through a review of some of the things that you've known before, but then we're going to go beyond that. We want to show you something about your world, that you do not now know. But it is something that you MUST know because it is important at this time that everyone of you have this information. It will give you a vision of the FUTURE . And the good book -- which is the written will of the Father -- says: "Without a vision people perish . " And we don't want people to perish . We want them to know what to expect so they can be ready for it. If you know what is going to happen you can cope with those things better, can't you ? All right . We're going to look into this situation tonight and find out what is going to happen.

On Chart #1, page 10 , we have 2 cubes. They the sun of represent our solar system and the sun of the solar system just ahead of us. We are told that in the density we live in there are more than 40 billion suns. And the INFINITE LIGHT source, or the source of intelligence represented by this line, comes right through this cube of the suns. This is known as the Infinite Light - line of inspired supreme intelligence , or the SUBSTANCE of FAITH . Have you ever heard that faith is a substance ?

Faith has nothing to do with "believing " . It has never, ever had anything to do with believing , because it actually is a SUBSTANCE . In this substance everything must be ALIVE . It must be full of life and light intelligence . In the substance of this faith there could be no transitory period that we know of as DEATH , because in this substance there is all life , all health, all happiness , all knowledge . And there is that ALL - SEEING INTELLIGENCE , which is the intelligence which cometh down from the Father of Light as a gift unto all mankind.

Now every good gift and every perfect gift cometh down from the Father of Lights , and it's the Father of Lights that gives us intelligence and the substance of faith. Each one of us has a MEASURE of this faith, so that we may have the amount of INTELLIGENCE that we do have , and so we may have the amount of LIFE that we have.

This gift of LIFE - INTELLIGENCE vibrates in the frequency of eternity . Time is only eternity slowed down. Time is eternity slowed down in vibration. That's what the brothers upstairs tell us.

This Infinite Light intelligence passes through the cube of the sun, for the sun is a cube. Every positive element is a cube. On this world we have 3 positive elements: salt, gold and silver . Reduced to a minute state each one of them are a cube. This Infinite Intelligence passing through the cube of the sun is broken up by the spherical action of the sun[2] and forms into the rivers of the waters of life , that are divided into 4 streams.

And actually the substance of faith that is passing through is the trunk of the TREE OF LIFE . It is not a tree of life, because there's only one tree. It is the trunk of The Tree of Life, and the Infinite Light -lines that radiate from that Tree , both positive and negative , are the branches of the Tree of Life . And we -- coming off of the branches of The Tree of Life or that Christ Vine -- we're some little branches out on there somewhere, because we all have a measure of that same substance which is called faith.

The speed of light , on the positive side is 186,000 miles a second. On the negative side it is 202,000 miles a second. If we were on course with Infinite Light -- if we were halfway between the positive and negative sides where we should be on course , it would be impossible to generate one watt of electricity . Because in

---

2.Photos taken of the sun show its outer envelope or photosphere but fail to show its actual configuration beneath that envelope.

generating electricity all we are doing is pumping electrons from the negative side at 202,000 miles a second through a vacuum to the positive side of 186,000 miles a second, tending to balance these, hence we have ELECTRICITY . But if we were on course, we would not need electric power, and the speed would be 199,000 miles a second.

Chart # 2 on page 11 shows the sun of our solar system . We'll just show you a portion of the Tree of Life . Our world is on the negative side over here, about 17 degrees out of course with Infinite Light . In the Bible in the 82nd Psalm and verse 5 it tells you that: "all of the foundations (plural) of the earth are out of course. " All of them are out of course. You say, well, what do you mean by all the foundations of the world? It must be a lot of little foundations we call people. No. That may be a metaphysical viewpoint, but the Bible says in the 89th psalm and the 11th verse that : " The heavens (plural) are Thine, the earth also is Thine (singular) and as for the world and the fulness thereof, Thou hast founded them more than one world."

And I've got a clue for you. All the stars you see in the sky , and all of the planets , no matter how high a degree of intelligence they may now have, are one day going to express much higher intelligence . " How do you know, Dr. Halsey ? " I know for this reason, that all things which are seen by your physical vision are temporal , or temporary. And things which are not seen are in that substance of faith which is ETERNAL .

Now, you say, we don't care too much about this thing that you call being "eternal" , or having to "drink of the waters of the fountain of Life. " Don't kid yourself . There isn't one of you here who wouldn't spend the last thing that you possessed in the world, to live one day longer.

But let me tell you. I'm showing you the way tonight , and some of the things that are ahead, where you're not going to live just 1 day longer or 1000 years longer ; but you're going to come into that eternal FOUNTAIN OF YOUTH where you're going to look like what you're supposed to look like in your own mind, ALWAYS . And that's going to be beautiful! If everyone is going to look like they truly hope to look in their own mind, they are going to be beautiful, aren't they ? And they are going to be handsome.

Over here (Chart #2) on a line with the substance of faith we have an object that is called SHANCHEA. Shanchea means "earth- child" . It was also known as the Garden of Eden, and as the New Jerusalem . It is the City Foursquare . It is all the same place . It is ON COURSE with Infinite Light , and we should be very happy that it is on course with Infinite Light because every prayer that we offer that goes higher than the ceiling must go through the crystalline foundations of this New Jerusalem in order to reach the Infinite Light intelligence of our Father Whose name is YAHVEH.

You're going to see some things tonight , some of you, that you've never seen before. When you say a prayer, you say: "Yahveh, in the name of Yahshua (or Jesus)" and there the connection is made to the intelligence and back and forth; and there is the conversation that has meant so much to you in so many instances. Before the Flood, before the time of Noah, this world was not as it is now. Before the Flood, there was a vaporous canopy around this world just like there is around Venus now. Oh yes , in Genesis 1: 6, 1: 7 it says, the waters were divided from the waters and in the midst of the waters was the FIRMAMENT of the heavens. The firmament of the heavens had an overlayer of substance which happens to be what is known as our oceans now. It was a positive - charged , vaporous canopy around the surface of this world . It was like an eternal, ethereal bow. Not a rainbow, because at that time it had never, ever rained upon the surface of the world. But magnetically , water came out of the ground and watered the whole face of the land in the cool of the day , which was on this side of the world away from the sun.

It was not in the cool of the evening , because there was never any evening there. Why not? Because there wasn't any CRUST on this world to blanket out the light of the proton or sun in the center of this planet . Oh yes, there are people who live in the center of this world. No, I haven't see these people , but I know they exist for two or three different reasons. The best reason that I know of is because the Bible says there are people who live in the INTERIOR of the world. Because this world , like every other creation of the Father and of His Elohim, or His family , is HOLLOW. Every one of them. In Revelation, the 5th chapter , verses 3 and 13, it speaks not only about the people above the earth which are the SPACE PEOPLE , and of the people on the earth -- which is us -- but it speaks about the people who are IN the earth.

When we lost this vaporous canopy, we lost 1 element out of every electron on the surface of this world. It is important for us to know that before the time of the flood, even though this world was about 17 degrees out of course with this Infinite Light intelligence , which is the substance of faith, people lived to be about 1000 years old. Each generation was named. Methuselah was 969 -- that's pretty old. Enoch was 335. And when their job was finished (building the pyramid) they LEFT here. They found favor with the Father . And they had means of going and so they departed .

Directly before the flood, people that were born 500 years before the flood , they only lived a little while after the flood. Even those who were on the Ark of Noah did not live too long . Directly after the flood, the generations of Abraham were only about 160 years old. Something was lost.... something that the vaporous canopy did for directing that Infinite Light to everyone on the surface of the world ... something was taken away. And the lifespan was cut from 1000 years down to about 160. And as the old debris (from the Maldek explosion) kept building up on the surface of the world , and it drifted a little bit further out of this Infinite Light source, the whole life expectancy table came down to where one time it was only a little bit better than 32 years , did you know that ?

It's coming back up, because this world is being RE - moved. It's been moved once. Anything that's going to be "RE " anything , has to have already been moved once. This world is going to be RE - moved like a cottage 存 -- which is a dwelling place of people -- and it's coming back to a position of being re- established ON COURSE with INFINITE LIGHT.

And I'm glad, because there are about 3,600,000 craft around the surface of this world, that have this world in their force-field NOW, and they are moving you in a direction that you cannot move yourself . This world is traveling 186,000 miles a second, and anybody here that thinks he can change the course -- slow it down or speed it up -- stand up.

No, you can't do it. But you're in good hands, and I'm glad that you're in good hands, aren't you ? Now I have something to tell you regarding the purpose of PYRAMIDS . The people of Enoch, 25,830 years ago built the great pyramids all around the world, all the way around the world. Oh, you say, I know about pyramids in Mexico and Egypt, but where's the rest of them?

Don't kid yourself . There are pyramids in California and I've visited a couple of them. Many of you people know exactly where they are, and if you don't, after the lecture I'll be glad to pass this information on to you so you can visit them yourself .You walk up on these pyramids and you seem to lose the consciousness of everyday , trivial things . And the magnification of this Infinite Light seems to grow greater , to where I doubt that when the sun is in the right declination and zenith, that you'd be able to get to the top of one of these mysterious pyramids .

The Indians in the area of northern California found one of these pyramids at

Snakehead Point near the North Fork of the American River , and they think the thing is haunted because for some reason they can't get close to it. They say, "There's something there. It stirs us up, makes us dizzy. We can't get close to that pyramid ... we can't penetrate it !"

Well , there is your natural man. The scripture says the natural man cannot understand spiritual things because spiritual things are spiritually discerned. It isn't meant for them to get in there. But I'll tell you, there are people like you and you and you and all of you, that are able to go to the base of this pyramid and climb and increase their INTELLIGENCE about all of these things . Pyramids act as a collector of the Infinite Light.

The Great Pyramid of Gizeh was a pilot model, where the Supreme Architect of the Universe allowed to be recorded every declination of the sun that this world will ever pass through , until it was again placed ON course with Infinite Light . Recorded in the archives of this Great Pyramid was all of the calculations for every other pyramid that was going to be built around this world, and there was a great calendar written in stone. It was a calendar to show just exactly WHAT was going to happen WHEN and WHERE ; and it was built by people who had an architectural knowledge from the Supreme Yahveh Himself. You'll find that this Great Pyramid , and all of the other pyramids , were built by the ancients for a very specific reason.

The pyramids -- all around the world -- were built to take the place of the vaporous canopy that was going to come down (and did come down) in a " Deluge of Rain " for 40 days and 40 nights at the time of the Flood when this world TURNED UPSIDE DOWN... and it's upside down now. But these pyramids collected this Infinite Light and brought it to the proton in the center of the world, which is a tiny sun in the earth's interior , to keep this world ALIVE . So you see these pyramids are exceedingly IMPORTANT.

Why The Tower of Babel was Built

The Tower of Babel was built in order to reach out to this Cosmic Light source that they were becoming out of course with. In the Book of Jubilees , which is one of the Apochryphal books excluded from the Bible , regarding this it says : "In Shinar, eastward from Ararat they went to build a tower to ascend to heaven... " The tower was built between the cities of Asshur and Babylon . It took 43 years to construct it and reached a height of 5, 433 cubits . Since 1 cubit = 18 inches, we see that the Tower was more than a mile high . This tower was quite a structure and was built on the magnetic lines , which served to strengthen it.

The 82nd Psalm in your Bible will tell you : "All of the foundations of the earth are out of course. " They were out of course with this infinite light . So the people (sons of Noah) building this tower were trying to build an antenna to reach back into this INFINITE LIGHT SOURCE, because they knew that their knowledge was waning. They missed it and so they were reaching out physically to retain that thing by means of this tower.

But the tower was causing the world to TIP even more greatly . So for this reason, the Space Brothers when they came, caused the tower to be thrown down. The throwing down of this Tower of Babel produced a terrific " seismic shock wave" in the strata of the earth when it impacted , and the repercussions of this shock caused fault - lines to slip and move considerably in a wide radius from ground zero where the tower fell . By confusing the language of the builders , the outer space people succeeded in halting work on the tower. Then they wisely toppled it over.

Why Evil is Intensifying in these End- Times.

Now let me say a few words about Satan, and his race of disembodied spirits , who are of course the lowest of all creatures . Both Satan and the evil spirits are the disembodied spirits of a race of men and women that once lived in the immediate, previous creation on this earth. Now listen. They are earthbound, and they are the only disembodied spirits in all of the universe. The people on other planets don't have to put up with them . But on our planet , those disembodied spirits are here as prisoners . And they are numbered, according to our space brothers... 900 million, billion of them. That's quite a few, isn't it ? 900 million, billion. Imagine that number of disembodied, earth-bound entities. They inhabit the air , or the atmosphere around the earth , and they seek embodiment and often obsess or possess the minds and bodies of men and women on earth. Actually , their present dwelling place is in the "attic darkness" above this world.

Attic darkness is found on the night side of the earth, or that side which is opposite the sun. You have daylight on one side of the earth and darkness on the other side . This darkness becomes more dense and more more dense until it becomes what is known as "outer darkness" . It is mentioned many times in your sacred texts. Bright daylight extends above the earth about 100 miles , and then the sky becomes a deeper and deeper blue which merges into a purple and eventually black. The stars are clearer and brighter as you move farther away from the surface of the planet . It is the resistance that the surface of this world (and its force- field) offers to the penetrating rays of the sun which gives you the light that you see on the day side of the world and call DAYLIGHT . Daylight is caused by this resistance.

Negative entities hate real light . Satan and all disembodied spirits , all 900 million, billion of them, actually belong in the outer darkness. But they attempt to transform themselves into "angels of light " . They try to fool people , because they will do anything they can to take something that does not belong to them, for a possession . Their aura -- listen to this -- you people who see auras -- is always black, or a dirty green, or a dirty , bricklike color. These disembodied spirits often glow as a deceptive light .

Michael, the Archangel , with other angels of Yahveh, have been in a battle. And don't you think that they haven't been fighting . They've been in a battle with the Satanic forces , and they are clearing the air . Satan and his demons at this minute are forced right down onto the surface of this world, because the air above is being cleared. They are being forced right out of their habitation. They are coming right down here and their force is becoming stronger all of the time , because they are being forced out of the place that they normally would be occupying.

Here is a scripture : "The devil is come down unto you, having great wrath, because he knoweth that he hath but a short time. " -- Revelation, the 12th chapter , verses 7 through 14.

Now our job at the present time is to release and set free all the people that Satan and the devils have bound with disease and insanity , and to bind the devils with the strong chains of truth. Because truth will set the people free, it says in Revelation the 20th chapter and the 2nd verse. In the ENDTIME period it is especially important that you be freed of these entities.

As magnetism can occupy the same place as a piece of steel , so can a disembodied entity occupy the same place and the same space of one of you people or any people in the flesh . They can literally occupy your body with you. Now, there is something about this that has never before been brought out, at least I never heard it. But it was brought from "upstairs " down to us to make known how serious and important this thing is . For instance, I talked to a lady in Kansas City , Mo. , not long ago.

She said, "Every night something happens to me. I feel something that just gives me chills all over. It's a terrible thing . I take a breath and it just feels like something jumps inside of me. Then I do mean things , I do crazy things , and when I want to do one thing I turn around and do something else. It's just like somebody else was inside, just taking me over."

And that's exactly what was happening to this lady . The Master said, when he sent the 70 out to minister , " Now, I've given you authority to do things . You go out and teach the good news, that the kingdom that is of heaven is going to be established here on earth. " All right . They did so, and came back and said, "Master, we're just tickled to pieces that we have power over the devil . We can cast these demons out of people !"

He answered, "You'd better rejoice that your name is written in the Lamb's Book of Life . You are covered with a surrounding LIGHT to where they can't jump into you because if they could they would certainly destroy both your body and your soul."

Inside of the Great Pyramid of Gizeh , they used to take the Pharoah who had passed on from natural causes, and they put him on a bed that was built just like a chariot that was going into a heavenly place . Remember ? You have seen pictures of the Pharoah. They'd walk him into the king's chamber and set him down where this Infinite Light coming down was concentrated on him. The only object in that room was the Coffer made of granite , and it was situated , amazingly enough, at the exact MAGNETIC CENTER of the Great Pyramid . The granite Coffer had no lid , and when the body of the Pharoah was laid in it, the lines of Infinite Light -force focussed perfectly at that spot. The Light - lines penetrated his body completely.

Now, he was not a religious person. He was of the earthy people . So far as religion was concerned, they were paganistic in all the things that they did and they cared nothing about anything higher because they were unable to discern it. Spiritual things are spiritually discerned, isn't that so? But they were of the natural races and they could not understand the spiritual things . They did, however, retain some of the knowledge that had been carefully documented by the " Initiate- priests " that had preceded them. A secret knowledge of how to restore human life , was known to them.

So, even though he had no spiritual substance about him, when he was taken into the king's chamber , they were able to bring him back to life[3] by placing his body in the granite coffer where he would receive a full charge of Infinite Light - force . The concentration of that Light was so great that after a few minutes he would

---

3. This is conditional. No return to one's body is possible if the Silver Cord has become severed .

awaken, stretch out his arms , rise up and put his feet on the ground and walk right out of the place -- full of LIFE .

Seeing this , the people began to worship him as God. This went on as a practice through many Dynasties of the Pharoahs , until finally one got to noticing that the restorative power of the Great Pyramid seemed to be lessening . He didn't know why it was becoming a weaker force , but he sensed clearly enough that it probably would not work for him and would not be able to restore him to life when the time came for him to die.

He said, "When I go the rest of them are going to have to go too ! " , and he gave orders that the pyramid should be SEALED UP at the time of his death, if it failed to revive his life spark . Well , it did fail -- probably because the natural magnetic anomoly upon which the pyramid had been built , had shifted a few critical degrees . Also, the super- solar influence of the greater sun Alcyone of the Pleides -- the sun behind our sun -- was no longer powerful as it had been in previous times . Time was once when the pyramidal force would do many things . It would open the THIRD EYE of the Initiate almost instantly . It would turn on all of the psychic powers, and it would even -- if certain conditions were observed -- restore you to life after you had died. But now it was different. The Pharoah remained dead, and the pyramid was sealed. But his body was buried elsewhere.

The Resurrection Light -- if you want to call it that -- failed because our planet had gotten so far off course from that life source. But listen ! A time is coming very soon when that same Light will be just as strong as it was 26,000 years ago, because our world is being RE - established back on its true course. This power of the Resurrection Light is destined to be restored to man here on this planet . We are being put back ON COURSE with infinite light . But watch out. When this infinite light is concentrated upon even a diabolical person or an entity whom we would term the lowest of the low, when they come into the center of this light they will also be resurrected because there can only be LIFE - that quick ! -- in that in- -- finite light because it is LIFE - GIVING. Why in the world would anybody ever want to resurrect that, and what happens if they DO?

If there is a disembodied entity (from the outer darkness) trying to get in, or if has somehow already gotten in, what is going to happen? Let us say that we've come to the time when we will receive a full concentration of the Infinite Light forces upon us, and say that we have 2 entities in us... what is going to happen? They're going to be resurrected, just that quick , and they're going to come back into the fullness of what they were created for by this substance of faith, which is hope, right ? So --

can 3 things of life matter occupy the same place ? No! That would destroy all 3 of them, wouldn't it ? Now here, just think about this.

Can you imagine people literally EXPLODING, because they would have a resurrection coming forth of other entities that are within them the same time that they would have their illumination. This is an important thing . I'm not saying this to scare people . I'm saying this to wake them up and let them know what's going on. All right .

We have two times . We have the time of this world , and we have HIGH TIME . This second phase of time is the time which the heavenly angels set, wherein things should be accomplished . This high time is known as just that -- HIGH TIME . It is high time to awake out of sleep , for now is our salvation nearer than we believed, it says in Romans 11: 11-12.

Now this may seem a simple little thing . But I wanted you to know, that according to the scriptures the 7th resurrection , or the last resurrection, would be for the disembodied entities. It literally would happen that way. And those entities are supposed to be taken and held in one place . They are supposed to be bound by the chains of truth . How can you bind anything by the chains of truth ? Truth will be a GATEWAY that will shut out the entities from entering into a temple that they do not own. They will still try to get in, but you will be a strong tower against them. And by using the sacred name: YAHVEH , in the name of Yahshua (Jesus) , then you can speak the word and surround yourself with an impenetrable light which they cannot enter into. For the name of Yahveh is a strong tower.

At the time when you come into an Infinite Light , which is all life and all intelligence , you may look around and see people just coming " all to pieces " because they are being literally destroyed by those who were trying to inhabit the same vessel . Oh yes. How many of these disembodied entities can get into a person? One or two ? No. The Master called out as he saw a person who had some of these entities in him. And he said, "What is your name? " The other answered and said, "My name is LEGION, for we are many. " Isn't that what he said?

Do you know how many a legion is ? 6,000. Entities are usually in a minute point form , but under the influence of infinite light they might be suddenly expanded in size. The Bible says that literally they will be resurrected. You've seen people congregating in one place at a Convention? We find that entities also love to congregate. Can you imagine what would happen to a person who is harboring 6,000 entities if they suddenly came into the focus of the infinite light ?

CHAPTER 3
You Know ALL Things
◆

All things that were ever contained are contained within YOU. You know all things . And the very fact that you do know all things , makes me think it's about time we begin to UNLOCK some of these things . Because we have a challenge at our door. We have a challenge for the very safety of all mankind. It's pointed out that what we have always feared would be the Armageddon of this world , would be a fight perhaps between the Communists and the free nations of the world .

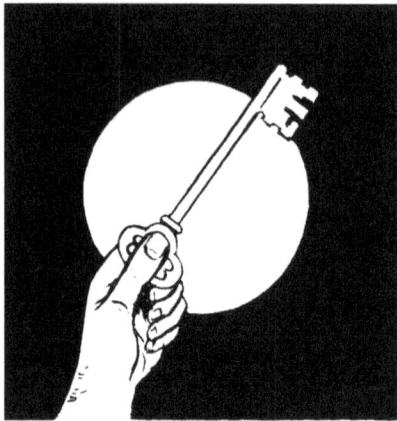

But it is coming down to where it is more than that, because it is a fight between the dark forces and the light forces . That is the way it is figuring . It's coming out strongly in that way.

We have been given a God- given heritage that is written down deep upon the table of our hearts, and everything that is ever to be known is contained within our consciousness because we were in the beginning with the Father. Do you believe that ? Genesis 2:1 says these were the generations in which the heavens and the earth were created, and all of the hosts of them. And the Lord was speaking to Job out of a whirlwind and said, "Job , where were you when I laid the foundations of the earth? "

Job didn't know. But we have come to the knowledge of the scriptures , and our understanding has been awakened by the very spirit of our Father for us to know that we were together with Him in the beginning . And in the beginning was the word, YAHVEH , which is His name. And all things were contained in the infinite mind that was given unto His sons and His daughters who were built in the image of the Father Himself . When you were built in His image , you were not only built in the image and stature and in the likeness of His body , and in the likeness of His features, but you were also in the likeness of His mind and intelligence , from the beginning .

You have passed through many, many phases of life since that time, even according to the Bible. But all things have been with you from the beginning in your soul and in your mind, which is the real you on the inside. Now it is written that flesh and blood shall not inherit the kingdom . But your MIND and your SOUL will inherit once again , the kingdom . And you are going to be redeemed, and it is not possible to redeem something that has not been pawned. You're going to go back into that intelligence that you once had. And it's written that it will happen soon, for in the end of this Age it says that all knowledge shall be INCREASED in the earth. Why?

Because YAHVEH says, "I will pour out My spirit (which is His Infinite Light) upon all flesh. " The Infinite Light is the source of all intelligence, for our Father is the Father of Lights . Now if you have a gift , I don't care what the gift is , if it is either good or perfect , it comes from this source of Infinite Light . For every good gift and every perfect gift cometh down from the Father of Lights . It comes from this Infinite Light , infinite intelligence source, right from HOME. If they would ask any one of you if you are home, you say "No, I'm just passing through here. I'm a stranger and a pilgrim . " If they ask you "What are you doing here?" "I'm learning things , but I'm not home! "

Well , the thing to realize is that you know all things , and to wake up and find out why you are here, and that you do know all these things and that they can be UNLOCKED . You know all things and I cannot teach you anything , not anything at all . This is an absolute truth. But I can stir you up, and bring to your conscious mind the things that you know, and by doing so I may be able to encourage you to put all things that you know, in PRACTICE . The Bible says , " You have an unction from the Holy One and you KNOW ALL THINGS. I have not written unto you because you know not the truth, but because you KNOW it. I am UNLOCKING this thing in you, says the Father. " That's in First John , 2:20-21.

You have an unction from the Holy One. You have that unction already , and you know all things . This is a fact and the absolute truth that you know everything . Now you say, I see a person and they say "I know everything " . Well , that was an absolute truth that they told you but they're not conscious of everything they know, do you see? When they come into the understanding that they can do things -- with the power and the might that has been given them to operate from the Father of Lights -- they say: "Isn't this wonderful! " Sure it's wonderful. That's just one thing that was UNLOCKED, that they didn't know was possible to them.

But it's written in the word that how many things are POSSIBLE to him who believeth? "ALL THINGS" ! Well , what does BELIEVE mean? I'm going to show you in a little lesson, exactly what believe means. I'll reach into my pocket and pull out all of my money. I have 25¢ here. Now, I want to be a banker . I want to be a banker. I have a communication with the Father to make my wants known. So I say, " Father, YAHVEH , in the name of Yahshua, make me a banker. " All right , now I've asked, haven't I ?

Now, He says if I will believe, I shall be that thing . Didn't He say that? So I take one step out of the place that I was in when I wasn't a banker, over to this new place that I'm going to be living in. So I declare unto you that I am now a banker. My capital is now 25¢.

Who wants to do business ? That is believing . If you believe that you have a thing , you shall have that very thing . That is beliving or to be living that very thing that you desire. That's what believing really means. It doesn't mean conjuring up your mind to accomplish something that simply wouldn't be possible in that way. Often you say, "Well, I believed. But it just didn't happen. " That's because you didn't put yourself fully into the place of LIVING it . Here is the way the Bible explains this knowing all things . "The anointing which you have received of him, abideth in you and you need not that any man teach you, but the same anointing teacheth you ALL THINGS, and is truth and is no lie . And even as it has taught you, you shall abide in him. " This is First John , 2:27.

Now what does it mean to be ANOINTED ? To be anointed does mean something very definite . In order to come into this knowledge -- - to be taught not of men -- we must know something more about what being anointed means. The word "Christ " (Christos) is a Greek title and means " the anointed one" . The word in the Hebrew is "Messiah " and also means the anointed one. YAHSHUA, which is Hebrew for Jesus , became Jesus in 240 A.D. , when they translated the Hebrew into Greek. Yahshua was anointed when he was 30 years of age. Here is the account of this in the holy scriptures : "And Jesus , when he was baptized went up straightway out of the water . And lo, the heavens were opened unto him, and he saw the Spirit of God descending like a dove, and lighting upon him. And lo, a voice from heaven saying , 'This is My beloved son in whom I am well pleased . ' -- Matthew 3: 16-17.

The spirit of God never left him. And thus his mind was obsessed and his body was possessed by the very spirit of God. It was obsessed and possessed by the spirit of God when he received this anointing . His body and mind and soul and spirit became the home of God. It became the home of the indwelled Elohim. That was the anointing. And from that time onward he was the Messiah , or the anointed one. The Christ means anointed one. In him, in Christ or in the anointed one, dwelleth all the fullness of the Godhead bodily . And mark this next sentence carefully ...

You are complete in him, when you have received your anointing -- not the same anointing that came upon him, but a like anointing . You are to be an heir and a joint - heir with him. The thing that he experienced , you can also if you will tune in to this higher source. When you receive this Infinite Mind, or this attunement or at- one- ment with the Father, and you are tuned- in, you have turned the dial of your consciousness up to where it says: "YAHVEH " . When you begin to hear the voice of the Father come in on that frequency , and you begin to feel something come over your body like an electrifying sensation to where it literally takes charge of you and fills you full, then ... you are COMPLETE . Until that time you are not complete , but it says that when this time happens you are complete in the Father because you've received of the Father all that He has for you at that time.

All right . Now I'm going to turn over to the book of John , the 17th chapter , verses 9 through 11. The Master said: "I pray not for the world, but for them which Thou hast given me for they are Thine. And all mine are Thine, and I am glorified in them. " What does GLORIFICATION mean? It means the intelligence of the Christ Mind has been put into them, so that they can KNOW ALL THINGS. "And now I am no more in the world, but these are in the world. And I come to Thee, Holy Father. Keep through Thine own name (which is YAHVEH) those whom Thou hast given me, that they may be one as we are. " There it comes, into one channel of vibration right from the headquarters down, so we can tune into this Infinite Mind and know ALL THINGS .

Now we'll go down to verse 20 through 26: "Neither pray I for these alone, but them also which shall believe on me through their word. " What does believe mean? It means to step out of where you were, and start to be LIVING that thing which you desire . " That they all may be one as Thou, Father, art in me and I in Thee. That they also may be one in us that the world may believe that Thou hast sent me. And the glory which Thou gavest me I have given them. " Is this past tense ? It's already been done. All you have to do is UNLOCK it because it's there. All you have to do is tune the dial. You could have a brand new radio, but if you never plugged it in and turned the dial , you'd never hear a thing .

Some of us have a brand new radio, but we've never plugged it in or turned the dial to hear the voice of our Father . All we have to do is DO it . That is believing ... to plug it in and turn the dial, because it has already been given to you. The light bill has been paid , you see? It's been dusted off. The dial has been set. A complete set of instructions as to how to operate it has been given to you. All you have to do is work it.

" Father, I will that they also whom Thou has given me, be with me where I am , that they may behold my glory (Christ Mind) which Thou hast given me for Thou hast loved me before the foundation of the world. O righteous Father, the world hath not known Thee, but I have known Thee. And these have known that Thou hast sent me, and I have declared unto them

Thy name (Oh yes , that was one of the main jobs of Jesus to declare the name of the Father, which is Yahveh) and will declare that the love wherewith Thou hast loved me may be in them and I in them."

I'll tell you this, that you were BORN. You were never created. You were born of your Heavenly Father and your Heavenly Mother and the Holy Ghost. Oh yes , born of the spirit -- isn't that what the Good Book says? The firstborn of many brethren was a king which is your elder brother. And if you don't think that there is going to be a spiritual people to stand up in government and in every other element of social life , standing for right and might in this world, then you'd better make a " retake" because you're going to be tapped on the shoulder by the forces from on high and asked if you will be a partaker with Him, in a Great Ministry .

The Ministry is going to be manifold. The Ministry is going to be the "Greater Works" which is helping to RE - move this world. Oh yes , it's been MOVED before. And do you know what's happening now? We're being RE - moved and re-established and we're coming into a position of being ON COURSE with Infinite Light . Before the flood the sun was seven times as bright as it is now. And it tells you, if you'll read the 30th chapter of Isaiah, that again the sun is going to be seven times brighter than it is now, and the moon will be as bright as the sun. That means that intelligence is going to be increased SEVENFOLD.

And where you have the equivalent of one of the seven spirits of God -- you know, the seven that are before the throne -- you're going to have ALL SEVEN of them! You say, well, I've had a couple of different kinds of baptisms already . Well , you just have five more to go through . So if you think you gained something in the first two, wait until you get through the second group of five . " Ear hath not heard and eye hath not seen, neither has it entered into the heart of man how GREAT these things are. " It would be impossible to describe! But I'll tell you, it's great enough that the "boys upstairs " , when they see somebody get on this right course and right path, they jump up and down for joy . It just tickles them to death, because they know that they're getting a brother and taking him right on through.

Tarna asked a question one time, and I thought it was kind of cute. She was talking to a friend of hers and said: "Say, don't any of the space people ever marry anybody down here? " They laughed and said, " That's what started the ball rolling to begin with -- that's the reason we're all in trouble! " But things are all going to be straightened out, and crooked roads are going to be made straight . I think that it's necessary that you know the kind of thing that we've been talking about, don't you ? I am sure you do understand these things , because ALL THINGS that you know are contained within you. Do you realize that it hasn't been too long ago, I believe it was Duke University that was having one of their tests in Hypnotherapy. They took a lady who was in her forties , and set her down in a chair and said, "Would you mind being a part of an experiment that we have?" She said, "No."

They asked, " Have you always lived in this city ?" "Yes" , "Do you speak any languages other than English ? " She answered, "No. I speak English only and I don't speak it very well. " They said, "Well, would you mind if we put you under hypnosis? " "I won't mind, if you tell me what you are going to do. " "You'll have to sign a paper . "All right . " So she signed the paper, and a few minutes later they had her asleep . They took her back to her childhood and beyond that.

They took her all the way back to the day that she was born. And they asked her, " On first opening your eyes , what did you see ?" She described a room that she was in, and she described a man with a red moustache talking to a young nurse. They asked, "Do you know what he is saying ? " And she repeated the conversation word for word, and it was filthy .

Then they asked her, " Now what are you doing ?" "I'm getting a bath" . And they took her all the way through that, and they took her into the crib . Then they brought her up to one week old and asked, "What are you doing now?" "I seem to be moving back and forth. I hear something that sounds like music. " "Can you tell us what it is ? "

She replied , "Yes . I hear an instrument playing in the other room. " They said, "Would you repeat what you are hearing ? " So she did. She sang a song in Greek, all the way through , and about four different choruses or verses of the song. Meanwhile, they were taking all of these things down. And afterwards they took her out of hypnosis , and they started checking on the things that she had said. They visited the hospital she had been born in, and they found that she had given a perfect description of a doctor who was still at the hospital . His language still hadn't cleaned up very much.

They talked to the lady's mother and asked, "Where were you when the child was a week old?" She said, "Well, I was having a little trouble, and they took me to the doctor's office to get some bandages fixed and to have a checkup . " "Who did you leave your baby with?" "I left her with the people upstairs in our apartment, which was a Greek lady who had a husband that played a violin. " They asked, "Do you know where these people are located? " "Yes, they live over on the other side of the city."

So they went over and located the Greek lady , and asked, " Do you sing Greek songs ?" She answered, "Oh yes . " "Do you remember taking care of a little baby about 40 years ago?" No, she didn't remember that. They refreshed her memory, and she said, "Oh yes, I kind of remember that. " "Do you ever sing Greek lullabys ?" , " Oh yes , I love them. I sing them to all my grandchildren . " They said, "Do you know a song that goes like this ? " She replied , "YES!", and she sang it for them, and it was the same song that this little child at one week old retained for all these years .

Your mind is capable of having everything that ever happened , ever , in the whole world , written on it -- and still contain enough room for everything that ever will happen to still be written upon the table of your mind. Isn't that something ? They have taken people under hypnosis , and asked them legal questions , that only the finest minds of jurisprudence could possibly know, and they got the answers just like that! Snap!

They've asked them technical questions and they've asked them regarding mathematical equations that are far beyond the understanding of the human being . It gets into the technology of IBM machines. And they said, "Well , let's see. I think it's this . " And they start rattling it off. Why ? Because you know all things , and it's proven that you KNOW all things . And if you want to prove it to yourself , come into a place of quiet meditation. Be still and KNOW. It didn't say, be still and listen. Or be still and expect. It says be still and KNOW, THAT I AM. Right here! There's only one person that you can call "I Am" and who is that ? I Am -- that's yourself , the divine one within you . Be still and know that I am the Elohim or God.

And when you come to the knowledge that you are , then you start to turn the dial, see? And you search back and forth... not up here (brain) but in the heart center. You'll tune into the infinite light - lines there , and when the focus is perfect , you'll hear the voice of the All - Father.

He'll be calling a new name upon you, and you'll say, "My, what a strange name! " But you write it down. It's your COSMIC NAME.

And if you don't want to reveal it to anybody , you don't have to.

But it's going to be yours . It always has been yours.

And it's the same as if He said, " This is your Cosmic Telephone number and I'll be calling you."

CHAPTER 4
Instant Space Travel
◆

This is going to be a little different tonight , because we are going to talk about two things : <u>angels</u> and <u>people</u> who have traveled instantly from place to place . Many people have traveled instantly from place to place , and scientifically you would call it Teleportation . For instance, we have some persons in this room who have traveled that way, and on several occasions I have traveled in this instantaneous manner, and my wife also. How physical were these travels ? Well , we took our automobile along !

My aunt is sitting in this room here. She's just a girl of about 80 years of age, and we were hurrying to Tacoma, Washington . We had a luggage trailer , and a pretty good sized load of groceries -- canned goods -- we were taking up there . And canned goods are heavy .

The closer we got to Mt. Shasta the snowier it got, and the report on the radio was this : If you have a truck or a bus with chains you can go on through . If you have an automobile with or without chains you cannot go, and especially an automobile pulling a trailer could not go because the roads were absolutely glassy slick with snow falling . So, we weren't going to stop. We just kept on going anyway, because we knew we had to go and the way would just have to be made for us. Authorities and powers higher than we were would have to be at work because we had to go. We couldn't stop.

So we drove and drove and drove. And finally I said, "I'm going to stop at the next service station and find out how much further we can go without chains" . My aunt said, "All right " . So we pulled into a service station on the right hand side of the road. I told him to fill the tanks and give me some anti-freeze and I asked: "How far can I go without chains ?"

He said, "35 miles" . I said, "Give me a set of chains. " We were go- (ing on through somehow. He said, "Where you going ?" "Well , 7 to push we're heading for Tacoma, Washington . " He said, "Man, you're on the wrong highway . " "I can't be, I've never gotten off of highway 99, " He said, "You're on highway 40. " "Well, how do I find 99?"

He said, " Just go down here half a mile and go through that tunnel two and a half miles long that you just came through , and then turn right at the first road and go 21 miles and you'll find your highway . " I looked at him and said, "I didn't come through a tunnel. " And I turned to my aunt, "Did you see a tunnel 2-1/2 miles long ? " She replied , "No, I didn't see one. "

So I said, "Mister, we didn't come that way. " He said, "You did, you came from that direction! " So I said, "O.K. So we came through a tunnel -- you say. " But none of us remembered coming through a tunnel. And we went back to where he told us. But during the time that we were, shall we say, "off course" , a warm rain came up and rained every bit of snow off the mountains, so that we didn't have to use the chains once . In other words , the weather was changed for us..

There have been other occasions when we were in one place , and we told people goodbye and headed for a distant town in our automobile. The next thing we knew we were stepping out of the car and greeting our friends in a town some 50 miles from our point of departure , and yet we had not experienced any sensation of a definite time lapse between start and stop. Instantly we'd traveled from place to place . The main thing we noticed at such times was that we had been exceedingly joyous , and would you say " spiritually positive" so that our vibrations were above the usual frequency.

Angels have a very definite bearing on things that are happening these days . Now, the ministry of angels (space beings who function in a realm of cosmic awareness that is normally outside or above the frequency barrier which closes in or presses in on the earth planet) is another one of the important things that were discarded by the church, and it must be restored. How many agree ? It must be restored, and I will first of all call your attention to an event in the Old Testament. Elisha and his servants were on a hilltop and the foot of the hill was completely surrounded by the Syrian infantry . The Elisha group was really outnumbered and they were in a bad way so far as a military standpoint was concerned. They were surrounded by the Syrian infantry and the cavalry and the artillery .

"Now the king of Syria sent thither horses and chariots and a great host and they came by night and encompassed the city about. And when the servant of the man of God was risen early and gone forth, behold, an host encompassed the city both with horses and chariots. And his servant said unto him, alas my master, how shall we do? And he answered , 'Fear not, for they that be with us are more than they which be with them . ' Well , he looked around and he didn't see anyone. He saw Elisha and he saw himself , and he thought , 'This man must be off his rocker because he says there is more with us than there is with them, and here we're surrounded ! ' If you were to go by appearances only , it looked hopeless for Elisha's group.

Elisha prayed and said, "Yahveh (which is the name of our Father) I pray Thee, open his eyes (not his outer eyes because he was already seeing with the physical eye , but he was asking Yahveh to react upon the servant's pituitary body and the pineal gland within him and let him see with the inner vision). I pray Thee open his eyes that he might see. " And Yahveh opened the eyes of the young man and he saw and behold, the mountain was full of horses and chariots of fire. "

Well! Chariots of fire ! What are these chariots of fire ? They are the same type of chariots of fire that have taken Elijah up. Oh, they didn't have horses on them, because they were chariots of fire . They were quickened to such a point that if you looked at them, it looked like rings of fire . They were the " swing low, sweet chariot" type of vehicle that are flying saucers. But it was out of the range of the mortal vision of the man in his physical self. He had to live spiritually in order to see with the inner vision, these chariots of fire , and it says there were many of them in the mountain. That mountain was full of them .... why ?

Consider an electric fan. You see that there are blades on the fan. And you can touch the blades. Then you plug the fan into the wall - socket, and it begins to turn at the rate of 1725 RPM. And you say, "I feel a real breeze rustling here, but I don't see any blades. " So you stick your finger in there, if you are foolish enough , and the blades would cut off your finger . Or they can spin 3000 or 3600 RPM and you wouldn't see any indication of anything being there at all . You might get a little noise, that's all .

And many times when these chariots of fire are around, you say, "It seems like I hear jingle bells , " because they do sound like faint little jingle bells or tinkling bells many times. It is a very shrill sound. My wife can duplicate that sound pretty good on the electric organ. It might be amplified a little bit as compared to the real thing , but we've has so many of them (UFO's) come over our ranch house on the desert that she's been able to copy it pretty good. So this is one way to tell when they're nearby .

We have a friend who lives on the desert near Yucca Vally , California. Her name is Dr. Mildred Bovee. Mildred Bovee came to our home one evening and said, "Now,

I came out here for a specific person. " I said, "You did? Who is this person? " She replied , "I don't know, but I want to see him in a flying saucer. " "Well," I said, "that's nice. " And she had brought a lady along with her from Rialto , California, an older lady . The older lady threw a startled look at Mildred Bovee and asked, "What did you say?" Mildred answered, "I want to see a flying saucer. "Oh, " said the older lady , "I don't believe in those things . I just don't! " So we walked outside to see what we could see at the edge of our yard , where we had kind of a corral there, and we started to LOOK UP..

Suddenly this lady who said she didn't believe in saucers said, "I don't know what's come over me, I'm so sleepy I just can't stand here. I'm just getting so drowsy , I'm afraid you'll have to help me into the house. Do you mind if I go to bed?" I said, "Certainly not. "

So Dr. Mildred Bovee took hold of her arm and took her into the house and tucked her in real nice, told her goodnight, and she went sound asleep (snap!) like that. So Dr. Bovee came back out into the yard with us, and I knew that we had one of these " chariots of fire " that many people do not see, close around, because I'd picked them up -- if you know what I mean. And we walked out to the edge of the yard and Mildred Bovee said, "I've always wanted to see one of these things , but I've never had an opportunity really , to see one close. I made a specific trip to come out here to see it." .

That is just the way she talked. I said, "All right , Dr. Bovee, if you will look at this very low cloud, right here, there is a craft within that cloud right now. And we are going to ask them to ionize that cloud and you watch, because it will lighten up brighter than day ." She said, "All right . " And we began to concentrate mentally . We didn't ask them out loud. We just thought a little bit, and guess what happened? That cloud lit up brighter than noon. And Dr. Bovee's chin hit her in the kneecap , and almost broke it because it dropped way down here! "My ! " she said, and she was speechless .

Now, many people could have been around, I'm sure, and never have recognized that anything would have been ionized there because these craft are of a positive polarity and they will attract negative moisture to them. And you will find, predominantly , that where people need help , and where people will believe that help is near, that right there will be craft. You may not see them with your eye until your inner vision has opened up, because in their frequency they have been QUICKENED like the spinning of that electric fan, to where the motion of the molecules in that craft are so great they are out of the range of our vision . Do you understand?

You will find that underneath the craft , if one were hovering anywhere, it creates a mighty rustling wind underneath. One night last week, we had a pretty good time here. And how many were here in this room when we had wind blowing , pretty hard? Because there was something upstairs over this place , we had wind blowing in this place , right here. All of the windows were closed and the doors were closed, but that's the sort of thing that is created by these chariots of fire .

Now this servant who didn't see anything around, when his inner vision was awakened and opened, he saw a chariot of fire around Elisha . And when they came down -- oh! there was more than one -- because it says "when they " . More than one came down because they were up above and came down to him. Elisha prayed unto Yahveh and said, "Smite these people , I pray Thee, with blindness . " Now, he didn't make them permanently blind. But whenever they (the brothers upstairs) would project their positive beam in strength upon these people , anything that was in their negative vision would not reflect , you see ? When they surrounded them with that light , even ordinary earthlight would not reflect. I'll tell you why.

For instance, this place that we call the "New Jerusalem " or Shanchea, which was the Star of Bethlehem, is a positive polarity craft. Its builder and maker is God which is the Elohim which is the heavenly family of the Father. It is 1200 miles square. It's a cube. It has 12 foundations and for a very definite reason. It's been orbiting this world for hundreds of years. It is a place that is established on course with infinite light , and therefore it is a communication center for all those on this world when they would contact the Father . They have to go through that mediation center , because we're OUT OF COURSE with infinite light . What happened?

On January 20th, at 4:20 a. m. , 1956, this positive polarity craft came within the atmosphere of this world which extends up for 26, 240 miles[4] . In case you didn't know it goes up that far, it does. And when it did it came between the sun and this world . And coming into this atmosphere it caused by ionization the atmosphere to LIGHT UP ten times brighter than the noon day sun, and this news item was carried in the Los Angeles Examiner and Times headlines for that day . It was on KFI and all the news medias. They didn't know what it was, but they reported it anyway.

4.Calculated by Cammile Flammarion, the great French Astronomer .

Previous to that, it came in between the countries of England , a portion of France and a portion of Ireland during the daylight hours. Now, one of the prophecies , I believe it's Hosea, says a time will come when the sun will be darkened at noon. They said a solid black fog rolled in. They could not smell it, couldn't analyze it, couldn't taste it, but it was absolutely dark. This huge , positive polarity craft had come between the sun and the earth, which blanked out all of the reflecting elements of the negative light , you see, by the positive force- field of this object .

It said that many people over there died of heart failure, and this was in all of our papers. It said that they could strike a match and could not SEE the fire , although they could be burned by it . They could light a lamp or an incandescent lamp and they could not see it , although they could feel the heat. They said it was a total darkness . If you want to call it a "blindness" you can.

Well , that's the same thing that took place when these chariots from above came down over this army. Elisha said, " smite the enemy with blindness" and the brothers upstairs did just that. They put the beam on on the Syrians , and it was of eternal elements, and it would not reflect their negative vision and so they went around in blindness. These are things of high science that they had available to them at that time which we have lost sight of now, but we're coming back into it.

All through the Bible, angels appeared to people and instructed them on which way to go, when to go, when to stop, what to do and the whole business, and they're beginning to do the same thing NOW. We definitely must have and we will have, the help of the angels of heaven to win the great battle against the dark forces in the LAST DAYS, and THESE ARE THOSE LAST DAYS. Listen to this scripture :

"And at that time shall Michael stand up, the great prince that standeth for the children of thy people . And there shall be a time of trouble such as never was since there was a nation, even to that same time. And at that time thy people shall be delivered... " Now the only way that you can deliver anything is to TAKE IT SOMEWHERE. If you were going to deliver a bushel of apples you couldn't do it simply by talking about it. You would have to take that bushel of apples somewhere in order to deliver it .

"At that time thy people shall be delivered, every one that shall be found written in the book, and many of them that sleep in the dust (symbolic of being in a subspiritual consciousness) shall awake, some to everlasting life and some to everlasting content. And they that be wise shall shine as the brightness of the firmament , and they that turn many to righteousness as the STARS for ever and ever, " it says in Daniel 12: 1-3.

Many people on the surface of the world , and many people in many different groups will tell you , "Don't believe what it says in the Bible, that certain things are going to happen, because they aren't. " And yet, they can look in the same scriptures , just 2 or 3 pages before the present time in the scriptures and find that it's already happened, which is a pretty good yardstick that it's accurate. Isn't that right ?

I would suggest that in reference to the finding out about the ministry of the angels that you would read Matthew the 13th chapter , verses 38 thru 43. Also read Revelation the 19th chapter , verses 11 through 16, because it will tell you the very job of the angels in reaping or PICKING PEOPLE UP for a housecleaning on this earth, when this crust that does not belong here is going to break up and be taken away. It is going to be cast off.

Now we've talked about angels and the people who are working for us behind the scenes, and many of them come right in here and they sit down on these chairs. It wouldn't surprise us at all , because they have been in our home and in our presence , and we know who they are and they know who we are and who you are . But, we want to find out about the abilities and capabilities of the people on this world , so let's look now at the performance of some of the other people and see about some of the men who have traveled instantly .

Out lord Jesus Christ , after his resurrection, was not limited by time or space. He was everywhere at the same time, it seemed, and could assume a material , physical presence not only in one place , but in a thousand places at the same time, instantly , if he desired to do so. And you say, "How is this possible ?" Well, it was done by a projection method. You say, "Well, that's impossible ! " Is it ? How many people watch television ? That is a mechanical means of duplicating something that is natural spiritually . That is a very minor copy of something that is available to every one of you, when you find out that it's a thing that's possible for you to do. I'll give you an example .

It was the 24th day of January , 1958 and I was in Long Beach, California to lecture. I was going to speak on PYRAMIDS for the very first time publicly . And I was waiting for the people to assemble in the hall. We had quite a crowd. And I was standing in the vestibule of the auditorium, when one of the lecturers of the Understanding group in Long Beach said, "Here comes Dr. Kinnaman, one of the foremost authorities of the world, on pyramids. He spent 11 years on Gizeh. Would you like to meet him?" I replied , "Yes I would." "Do you know him? " "No, I never saw him before."

So I was standing there like a bump on a log waiting for an introduction see? And he comes up and his face lights up and he puts out his hands and he says, "Dr. Halsey , I'm so glad to see you again ! I so enjoyed your lecture in San Francisco just a month ago tonight . I enjoyed the things you told me about the pyramids , " And he just went down the line on what I was going to speak about the first time that night . My chin began to drop , and I said, "Where was this ?" He said, "Don't you remember the hall?" and he went into detail about this thing . And I've got news for you, I haven't been to San Francisco for a year and a half! The 24th of December was Christmas eve and I was sitting with my wife and children around this organ in our house in the desert , and we were singing carols and having presents, just like Santa Claus, you see? But at the very same time, this man, Dr. Kinnaman was attending a lecture with others in San Francisco and they were hearing this very thing .

You know something ? We felt that was incredible , and we checked into it and guess what happened ? There WAS a lecture there on that date. What I want to know is , when is my other self or my reflection, due with the money? I don't recall ever getting paid for that San Francisco lecture!

Tarna L. Halsey,

Dr. Halsey's lovely wife. Tarna played the organ beautifully at Dr. Halsey's New-Age meetings although she never had a music lesson in her life . It is said that Tarna has almost total recall of a past lifetime on the mysterious planet Venus .

Dr. Wallace C. Halsey at his ranch. On the day this photo was taken the wind was blowing 20 to 30 knots per hour, yet this U. F. O. shaped cloud hovered above his ranch house for one hour. Photo is composite of two snapshots taken consecutively.

CHAPTER 5
What is Cosmic High Noon?
◆

Six weeks ago the scientists of the United States reported that the magnetic polarity of the sun is beginning to CHANGE.[5] They are beginning to measure that right now. It came out in an article in the Chicago -American. It was listed by the United Press International, and appeared in most of the newspapers of the nation. We are told by high authority , and we are reminded, that when the polarity of the sun begins to change it is an indication that the polarity of the PLANETS that are subject to this sun are also beginning to change . This is VITAL information.

We are UPSIDE DOWN. This world has been upside down since the time of 3 Noah -- since the very time of Noah! We 8 4 are coming to a time of "housecleaning " . 5 Not only are we coming to a time of house6 cleaning , but we are coming to the time of -- would you say , a RESURRECTION -- of this world ? Because we are told it is imminent that this world will suffer the greatest overall EARTHQUAKE that all history published anywhere has ever known. And at the time of this great UPHEAVAL , it will upset the systems of economy and the systems of government to such an extent, that people will not know exactly which way to turn.

These are absolutely serious times . At the same time that the upheaval is going on, there is a greater CHANGE being effected in all of our universe and I'm going to show you from the Charts , just what it means.

In February a year ago, (1959) we stated to you that we had been told that according to the Cosmic Clock it was 2 minutes until 12:00 O'clock . At that time we did not know what the Cosmic Clock was , nor did we know what 2 minutes to twelve was. But we have been told since, that it is not 2 minutes to twelve any longer. But it is less than 1/4 of a minute to twelve, and we have been told what the

---

5.The full and complete reversal of the sun's polarity actually occur- 40 - red between mid - 1957 and late 1958, according to Caltech scientists. .

Cosmic Clock is .

You will find (see Chart #3) that this is a vortice in which we earthlings live , and it is known by the name of "Contri" . And next to this vortice which is a density called the 3rd density , there is an overlap . We will call this "Blaau" and it is the 4th density . Our planet , and this complete solar system for 312,000 years has been traveling through this 3rd density . The speed at which we have traveled through this density has varied , because 55,000 years ago there was an UPSET or an UPHEAVAL which caused the planets of these different systems -- not only this one but the system behind us also -- and also the system in front of us, to be shaken out of its course.

Many of you people are Bible students , and I would like to quote a scripture to substantiate the world being out of course with infinite light power, or out of the place in the heavens that it should be. In the 82nd psalm in your Bible it states that, "All of the foundations (plural) of the earthare OUT OF COURSE. They are out of course with infinite light . We are coming to the place now -- and the only time when a world or a group of planets can be RE - moved from a position of being out of true course, to being RE - established in a position of light and "ON COURSE" . And that is when a group of planets or a solar system moves from one density to another density . We have been traveling in the 3rd density , which vortice is in the anti- clockwise direction and is of a negative polarity . The 4th density is in a clockwise rotation, and is of a positive polarity . At the present time we are in the "Arc of Cosmo" (Chart 233 #) which is coming into the overlap between the two densities .

Our climates are changing . Our conditions are changing . And not only are these things changing , but because of being in the influence of the 4th density , KNOWLEDGE is being increased in all of the earth. Not only here locally , but in ALL of the earth, knowledge is increasing . We have television now. We have telephones . We have automobiles. We have a great technology that was not available to us before because we were not in that high vibratory plane . We were not previously in the influence of the 4th density . But knowledge is being increased, and we're coming to the place very soon which will be the HEIGHTH of the rise -- as far as we can rise in this density -- which is the exact center of this "Arc of Cosmo" .

That can be pictured on the great Cosmic Clock as the heighth of the rise which is COSMIC HIGH NOON. And we're told that the hand is pointing to less than 1/4 of a minute to COSMIC HIGH NOON. At this time there will be an illumination of minds -- not brains but of minds - which is that infinite mind that dwells within each and every one of you.

You wonder ,"If all of these UPHEAVALS are coming , what about me and what do I have to fear ?" Let me tell you, that there is not a person in this place that has one thing to fear , because our brothers upstairs are working out the final arrangements of a plan to help you, because you do not know how to help yourself . It has also been stated that, in these END- TIMES, many things and many upheavals would be brought upon the children of men.

But it has been written by our great Father in His written will which is the Bible , that He would never put anything upon His children without at the same time giving them a WAY OF ESCAPE .

You will find at the beginning of this terrible upheaval , that there will be an increased knowledge on your part , and more action by the forces of light . En masse they're going to start to get a little bit bolder . Instead of being seen as " streaking through the sky " , or maybe slowing down and parking in mid-air for 3-1/2 hours and having the newspapers say, "Well, we don't know WHAT it was . It's an unidentified object , and it must just be an hallucination, you see ?", the UFO appearances are going to be stronger.

Even some of our science has advanced beyond their understanding , because recently in New York City the Society for Psychotherapy , I believe they call it, at Columbia University , tried a little "Bridey Murphy " type of experiment. They took a GROUP of people that had very little knowledge scholastically , put them under hypnosis and took them back, way back. In questioning one of the group, after having brought him way back on the time track , the interrogator unwittingly made a slip of the tongue and said to the hypnotized subject , "What WORLD did you come from, and what were you doing there before you came here? "

Now, he meant to ask "what country" but instead asked "what WORLD" . And the man said, "Well, I was riding about in a ventla, which in the latter times will be known as a flying saucer, and I dwell on the moon. " Now this is a matter of record in a University manuscript . And they said, "This man is having an hallucination. " But they believed all the other things he was able to bring out, because by probing into the Subconscious mind of that man, they were able to bring out formulas and answers to equations which only their advanced IBM machines were able to answer in a short period of time. This man was able to give them those answers. But to this one question, they said, "Well , we got into the HALLUCINATION department of his Subconscious because he's talking about flying saucers , and certainly there is NO SUCH THING. " Can you imagine that ?

The technology that is coming forth now is BEYOND science. We are told that we have 1000 days to spread infinite knowledge and infinite light , and to quicken the understanding of individuals like yourself . But on hearing you are also receiving a responsibility unto yourself , because you are expected to turn around and give the information out to some one else .

You say, "Well , if we're going to depend on them and they're going to do everything for us, then we don't have to do anything . Oh no. We're going to have to work TOGETHER , because this is a collective thing and you'll find out one day that His family is here. Now you may come from different homes but you're of the same family , and you all have to have breath in your nostrils in order to remain alive . And you're all depending on the great source of INTELLIGENCE and INFORMATION for your survival. And you are all "putty" in the hands of your higher brothers, for it is written that the angels have been given charge over you, and you are but a garden that is planted . A time is coming for a reaping , but you are going to help do some of the reaping .

I want to tell you that 20 clergymen from around the world were appointed to go into the Gobi desert recently . They were appointed to investigate a report that there was a person there who claimed to be GOD. This person was doing unreasonable things , called MIRACLES .

On going to that region of the Gobi, they said that they never saw such splendor as was contained in a certain palace that is situated there. Going into the palace they said they felt a compelling force and felt like they were drawn into a particular room. And going into the room they saw a great man, a big man, sitting upon a solid gold throne. Around this throne was the most gorgeous and magnificent carvings that you could ever imagine , and it did not look like it had been made by the hands of men, it was so beautiful and so wonderful. And they said there was a force within them that made them nearly sick at their stomach, but they felt compelled to bow down and to worship this extremely powerful person.

This man is claiming that he is God, and he is doing miraculous things . But we know and we are told that there is a certain person that is the God of this world. We are told that Satan is the God of this world, according to your Bible. Did you ever read that in your Bible?

And it is the opinion of some of these people that this person has come to claim a power. It is also the opinion of persons of higher authority that he will try to usurp your inheritance and take it away from you. And you will find that the forces of Darkness are at work throughout the world and even in Kansas City , Missouri. I mean this with all of my heart. Power is given unto the children of men, to combat these forces and it is written in the word, and I was reminded again this morning that it is written that all of you are made a little lower than the angels . But you are going to be crowned with glory and with honor. And if you do not know what the glory of God is of the Father that is given to you -- I will tell you. The glory of God is INTELLIGENCE .

And you are going to be given the intelligence to combat all of the forces of Darkness and all of the upheavals of the world , and the time when you will receive the intelligence is not far away. Because soon you're going to hear on the Cosmic Clock the great chimes of Time sounding . And with the sounding of that cymbal , there is going to be an illumination process in the minds of those that will diligently seek.

Our brothers upstairs said: "We have not asked to be admitted into the minds of people before. But very soon, we are going to ask to be admitted into the MINDS of people that we may give them guidance and direction , so that they may be crowned with their inheritance which is the intelligence of the Almighty ... because it is going to be INCREASED. "

For a period of several years , we'll be traveling past the 12:00 O'clock period . We will be traveling past, and we will be fighting two forces after we cross this time, because the VIBRATORY FREQUENCY will be INCREASED TO A GREAT EXTENT , and there will be a counter- action between the force of the 3rd density and the force of the 4th density . It will cause this world to ROCK . And in rocking , there will be much consternation and fear in the hearts of most people . But in your heart -- because you are going to be ILLUMINATED with a great knowledge and a greater intelligence, even an infinite intelligence -- you are going to have NO FEAR .

But you are going to be endowed with LOVE instead. And you are going to be the ones who are your brother's keeper , and freely you are receiving and freely you shall give , and raise them up to a HIGHER LEVEL .

I'll tell you this , that the time is coming and is here now, where information on technology is being given into the hands of people like you. Such technology as to

48

how to combat radioactive fallout , even in the face of an atomic attack. For it was written that the Father would not allow put upon you more than you could bear, or give you a position to stand in trial without making first a way of escape.

The brothers from upstairs at this time , are looking for people who are willing to roll up their sleeves and go to work. Because between now and 1963 the Clock will have sounded Twelve... and we will have passed this mark of Cosmic High Noon. You will have received a degree of ILLUMINATION according to the amount that you would let yourself receive . And you will have become aware of interplanetary vehicles -- ventlas , or flying saucers if you would want to call them that -- and most of you will have seen them . These things are realities and very IMPORTANT to you.

Into the hands of some of the UFO enthusiasts, who are all people full of love , those that we have met and we have met many thousands of them, you will find is given KEYS to technology . One of our group has been given certain information that has changed the whole concept insofar as the theory of ELECTRICITY is concerned. For he has been given information on a device to make objects WEIGHTLESS , to where he can place a given object in the air of the room any place that he wants, and it just remains there. He could move it over . It is not propelled , but it's weightless and could be propelled very easily .

What does all this mean ? It means that engineering science from a higher intelligent level , is coming into our midst to show the people that there is a great TECHNOLOGY and a great WAY OF LIFE that is once again being delivered into the hands of mankind on the surface of this planet. It cannot be metered, neither can it be piped . It cannot be sold. It is FREE . It is part of your inheritance. According to our science it is IMPOSSIBLE . But you are living in the day of IMPOSSIBILITIES !

Recently , before Christmas, we had stopped in Des Moines, Iowa. We were moving some things from Des Moines to the West Coast and we had some lectures scheduled there . For some reason -- and I know the reason now, I didn't know it to begin with --- we had trouble with the canvas on the luggage trailer that we were pulling . It just blew all around, we couldn't keep it tied down at all . So we stopped at Tucumcari, New Mexico.

Now mind you, our automobile carries a California license , and we were in New Mexico parked off of the highway . And as a matter of fact the car was pointed north because we'd gone around the block . Pretty soon a man came walking up through the town and although we didn't pay much attention, it is a small town and you can see people . He walked directly up to me and he said, "Hello! " I said to myself , "My , people are friendly down here. " But I felt something . So did my young son, Gary , who was with me.

Gary is 13 years old. He said, "Daddy, I don't understand this. I feel a sort of electrical charge . " Then the man spoke to me: "You're coming out from Des Moines, Iowa, and you're going to California . "

I raised my eyebrows a little bit at that, and replied , "Yes, that's right . " Then this man had a little conversation with me and he told me a few things I was glad to know about, because they concern all of us. And let me tell you, there are crises coming that are going to require your individual prayers . The outcome will depend upon your prayers (and don't you ever think that they don't count) and not only that, but if you will begin NOW to seek for contact[6] with the authorities from above - the forces of Light -- those who diligently seek are going to find .

Some of you may be thinking , "Well , gee. They're going to come down in a mist or a vapor , and they're going to look like a bunch of GHOSTS walking around. " NO -- they're not. They're going to come up --KNOCK , KNOCK ! -- on your door and they'll say: "Miss Jones , we know what you have a desire for, and you've said that you would do anything of service . "

You'll say, "Did I say that ?" They'll reply "Yes. " And they'll tell you exactly what you did say and they'll point out: "The time's come when we can use you. Are you still willing ?" And that will be your opportunity to go to work. They'll present you with identification so that you'll know without a shadow of a doubt, who they are .

We had an experience , not too long ago, where my wife and her girl friend were having quite a conversation. They were in a powder room, and you know how women will curl their hair and they'll talk. They were talking over a lot of things . Later on in the evening we went home, and we walked out into the yard . And a CRAFT came down very low, even low enough to where we were able to speak to the people in the craft . That is pretty low, isn't it ? And we thought, "We don't know these folks. "

They introduced themselves, which they always do. They tell you where they're from . They said , "We've seen the intents of your heart today -- and even your conversation. Would you like to hear the recording ? "

---

6. SECRETS OF HIGHER CONTACT, by Michael X,

"Oh yes ! " We were eager to hear -- right now -- anything they had to say. Then they played the recording back of the feminine conversation in the powder room. Do you remember that, Tarna ? It lasted for about 25 minutes. I thought that men got off and talked and gossipped sometimes, but let me tell you, THAT recording was really something ! They (the Space Brothers) know the thoughts , the intents of our very hearts -- all of us collectively -- and those thoughts and intents are being RECORDED . Everyone of our thoughts and intents is being recorded.

Many of the craft in this solar system and around this solar system are from the 4th density , which is a very high frequency . They are from that constellation whose sun is Arcturus . Do you remember reading in the Bible in the Book of Job -- I believe it's around the 39th chapter -- where the Lord was speaking to Job out of a whirlwind, and said:" Job , what do you know about Arcturus and his sons ?" And of course Job didn't know. But we know that these are the SONS OF ADONAI.

And we know that when the Sons of Adonai come into our midst, that many times we feel their presence but we do not see them . Now, you say, "Brother Halsey , are you talking about ghosts or spooks or spirits ? What are you talking about ?" I want to call your attention to one thing . In the 4th density they are in a higher vibratory frequency than we are , and they are established on an ETERNAL plane .

It is written in the great book, and in many great books, that things which are SEEN are temporal , which means TEMPORARY . But things which are not seen are ETERNAL . And you will find that the brothers of this solar system right here, are temporal , just like we are, for the greatest part. They are higher in intelligence because they are closer in to the infinite light source - closer -- to being " on course" . But they also look to higher brothers, and you will find that the Sons of Adonai are in our solar system now to help us, and many times you will feel their presence around you. You may even feel them put their hand on your shoulder or around your shoulders, though you do not see them, because they are eternal.

They are our higher brothers . And I'm not talking about anything that is unreal or DEAD or anything else. If we only knew the truth, we are SO DEAD NOW... that we could not possibly do anything to be more dead than we are . And even the Master when he was here said that we were (the masses of mankind that is) DEAD, and he told one of his disciples : " Let the dead bury their dead. " They didn't even know who was dead and who was alive . But we are now coming to a place of reality .

We are coming to a place of understanding . We're coming to a place of standing up and receiving our inheritance in light , from our brothers above. Let me tell you, it's a pleasure to talk to many of our Space Brothers. It is a pleasure to talk to that mysterious gentleman I talked to in Tucumcari , New Mexico. But at the same time, and my wife will tell you the same thing , when you have the privilege of a conversation with the being known as Ashtar , it is mostly listening ; and there's no monkey business at all . You feel just like the new recruit in the Army standing before an old- seasoned top sargent. You shake in your boots and say: "Yes sir ! "

And he'll tell you , "When I say to stand at attention, why don't you stand at attention?" Like the recruit would reply , you say, "Well sir , I'm standing at attention, but the underwear you issued me will not stand up! " (Because it's usually too big anyway, you see?) But I mean that we're coming to a place where the highest authority is taking a definite interest in you as individuals , and they're delivering into our hands means of escape from trials . But at the same time they expect you to turn around and pick up your brother, and say, "No matter what you are, no matter what you have been, I am your keeper . This is the way - walk you in it . "

If they turn and go another way, your responsibility has finished. Take no more concern there, but pick up another brother, and tell him the same thing . Because you are coming into the place of being little shepherds herding the sheep into a position of being evacuated for a time , when the final finale of this great earthquake takes place .

There's going to be a crackling loose, and the CRUST of this world is going to be repelled off the surface of this world into the bottomless pit which is endless space. It's going to keep on going . But about that time you're going to say, "I always wanted to ride one of those spaceships -- now I'm riding one! " And it's going to be kinda good to see what the old world looks like after that debris and crust has been taken off, and the New Earth has been established, and the oceans have come up and made a vaporous canopy above like our sister Venus has. Like John said, "Behold, there was a New Heaven and a New Earth . I saw no more sea.. " It went right back up where it belonged, as a vaporous canopy.

And when you come back down, you're going to see all of the kingdoms of this world that took millions of years to build , right on the original shell of this world, in all of their beauty and all of their splendor . And you will say, "Those are so gorgeous ! They're not built to last only 30 years and I don't see a single FHA sign ! It looks like they would last forever ! "

They'll say, "Yes , and here's your position over here and here's your position over here, and they're yours . "

In the midst of it , I look for a beautiful Temple to be built right on the original shell of the world , after this crust has been removed. And I do not believe it will be very long until this crust is removed, nor will it take long for the removing to take place when this world turns right side up. I will qualify this . Fifteen years ago, the lines of longitude between your magnetic north and south poles were 106 degrees apart . The world normally tips on its axis 1/2 a degree in 600 years.[7] In January , 1956, one bomb exploded in the South Pacific caused the world to precess enough to cause it to tip on its axis by 1-1/ 2 degrees , which is equivalent to 1800 years -- one little A- bomb! This is a scientific fact .

Right now, we lack very little of having the magnetic north and south pole lines coming exactly together -- converging -- and when they cross there will be a change of POLARITY . How close we are to this is determined by the change that is being effected upon the world NOW. Because you see the climatic changes that are taking place are unusual. This is pretty unseasonable weather that you're having here right now. And I understand they had sleet in Los Angeles the other day ! Things are CHANGING - the world is tipping . In 1956 in Fairbanks, Alaska, it rained for two weeks in January , something that had never happened in history .

And the very fact that the polarity of the sun is changing (and our scientists know it) is but a fact that the polarity of this world is changing , and we're beginning to turn now. And when we reach a critical point , then, the " tares " -- some of these boys who are setting up palaces in the Gobi desert and saying "I am God - fall down and worship me! " , that are represent- $ ing a destructive force of Darkness that has already caused one planet , the planet Lucifer - Maldek, to be destroyed -- the Space Brothers have said: "We'll gather up those tares , and we're going to haul them out of here first . "

But you people are going to have to stay around awhile to see that the final , final crop has been brought in and the last brother has been taken hold of by the shoulder and told: "Brother, this is the way that we're going to have to go, and here is the information that we have. We've received information from up above and now we're going to prove it to you. "

When they see that this is true, they're going to go right on in. And that is going to

---

7. The Lunisolar year, or Naros. It is the most perfect of periods and is precisely 600 years.

usher in not a Republic and not a Democracy , but a KINGDOM. A Kingdom is going to be re- established upon this earth, because each and every one of you happens to be a personal representative and an ambassador upon this world FOR THAT PURPOSE.

This world is crooked and is out of course, and we've said many things here today , and I think that we can qualify them.

You'll find that two words were left to you from the original confusing of languages at the time of the Tower of Babel . And this world being out of course and being crooked is but an example of ourselves ; for you'll find that one side of your body is longer than the other. We are out of balance, let's face it. We are out of course also, because we are partakers of all things with the INFINITE LIGHT of the world that we're an inhabitant of. But we are all going to be straightened up and so is our world going to be straightened up. This is in the All - Father's Cosmic Plans.

I want you to come into a knowledge of part of your inheritance. I'm going to give you the name of your Father that's been hidden, the Father , the Eternal Father of all heavens and all universes and all galaxies and all that there is . His name is YAHVEH. In this name is all-power; and it is a moving power and a changing power. It is written, "Whatsoever you ask in the name of My Son, (which is YAHSHUA in the Hebrew) that will I do. " The name has been given back to you.

There are many things that you as individuals are being depended upon to fulfill upon the surface of this world during these END- TIMES . Many individuals are ambitious and would like to take someone else's place , but I'll tell you, that no one of us can usurp someone else's position . Each and every one of us is a KEY and there is a LOCK for each and every one of us to open.

If you will seek for guidance from the higher forces , and ask for cooperation and to be of cooperation to the higher brothers , I promise you that your lives will change in a very short time.

CHAPTER 6
The Secret Name of God
◆

We're going to speak on the Sacred Name. Now, I'd like to state this, that in the very beginning of the implantation of mankind upon the surface of this world, all men spoke the SAME language . A pure language had been given to them, and all men spoke the same language . It was wonderful, the accomplishments that could be made through the VIBRATORY frequency and vibrational tone quality of each word. It commanded substance, or faith substance, to create that thing which they spoke .

They spoke the word. And when they spoke it through this knowledge they were able to draw all those elements together out of the ethers, that would create for them that very thing which they desired . They were able to commence LIVING that thing , and have it in their hand.

During the time that we all spoke the same language -- and it was a pure language that was given to us -- we could command things and we had the substance of INFINITE LIGHT available in full power to see that we manifested whatever we should say. And it is stated that the time is once again to come, when "thou shalt have whatsoever thou sayest ". But we can't do it now. Let's face it. If we could do that, we could speak into existence the things that we require in our life . We would put the manufacturers out of business because I'm sure our imaginations would build things better than we're able to buy them today .

When we came out of course with infinite light , it was like losing a priceless "treasure of Light " . There came a time when those who were upon this world then, knew that they were losing their higher " light consciousness" . They knew they were losing the intelligence of the Father which comes from the source of this infinite light . So they started building a tower which was the Tower of Babel, and you've read about it in the Bible. But if you really want to find out about it you'll read about it in the Book of Jasher which is mentioned in 2nd Samuel in your Bible and also in the Book of Joshua in your Bible , although it is not contained as one of the books of your Bible itself.

If they had been permitted to go ahead and work on the substance and the knowledge of the language of the infinite light by speaking those words, they would have accomplished the building of this Tower. It says that in the Bible . But that Tower was causing the world to become MORE out of balance, even to the extent that it was not prepared for. So the brothers upstairs said, "We've got to stop this . How? In two ways. We will throw down the Tower and we will confuse their language . " And they backed up this twofold plan with positive action . They confused the language , so instead of there being one language there were 2716 languages on the surface of this world, including all of the dialects that we know about. And that's a lot of different languages .

So the Tower builders could not get along together . They could not make themselves understood. When they would speak something , expecting that it would come into existence, the multi-languages wouldn't work because they were not pure.

Of the original language only 2 words have come down to us today , to have as a possession as a part of our inheritance. But these words are as " seed" for bringing back once again the other things that we are going to need. And what are these 2 words ? One is YAHVEH .

Now you will find that the original tetragrammation of this word is YHVH . But we speak the American version of the English language , don't we? And Y- H-V- H are consonants. Our vowels are A- E-I-O- U and sometimes W. So it makes this first word YAH (inserting the first vowel) and VEH (taking the second vowel) . Both syllables together spell YAHVEH .

In some of the translations that you will find, also in the new language or the sacred language New Testament which is available , you will find that it says YAHWEH . And the reason for this is , it is an English version translation from England where they use a "W" instead of the "V " , just like they use the "S" and call it SION instead of " Z" for the word ZION. That is the difference between the two translations . But nevertheless, this is one of the 2 words that have been given to you for an inheritance and to know.

You are to have it as a possession , not just to know but to use. How many of you people have used this word YAHVEH and seen miracles right in front of your eyes ? You're going to see some today if you've never seen them before . All right .

The second word that was given, still of the pure language for you to have as a possession is the word ELOHIM , which is the name of the family of YAHVEH . He gave these two names, His name and the name that He calls upon the family . And where you see in the Bible the word " GOD" - -- even where it is pronounced singularly , God -- it is taken from the word ELOHIM which is always plural and never singular . It's never singular .

"Our help is in the name of the Lord, who made heaven and earth. " It tells us that in Psalms 124:8. But we have not known His name. Yet the sacred name is absolutely essential to our survival in the END- TIMES of this age.

That name : YAHVEH, is the Divine Seal. It is very, very important for us to be sealed in the forehead with the sacred name which is YHVH (YAHVEH) . In Revelation 14:1 it says that those having their Father's name written in their foreheads are under protection . They are safe from the dangers which come in the END- TIMES . "The name YAHVEH is a strong tower: the righteous runneth into it, and is safe. " , according to Proverbs 18:10.

We should know both the name of YAHVEH and also the name ELOHIM , and we should use them. Why ? Because the title " Lord" that is now being used in the Bible , appears approximately 6000 times. And in nearly every case it is the title that has been SUBSTITUTED for the name YAHVEH . It has been substituted for the true name which is the one and only true name of our Father which art in heaven. The title "God" is used approximately 7000 times for the name ELOHIM . In addition to the titles "Lord" and "God" there are no less than 10,000 other titles in the Bible for YAHVEH and ELOHIM. 10,000 more titles that should have been relegated to these two original names, Yahveh and Elohim. But in their translation they have been changed. How on earth could this have been accomplished ?

You'll find that during the time of Constantine, about 335 A.D. , that it was made mandatory that Christians or the Early Church could come up and worship as they saw fit , even on an equal basis with the heathen. And when this rule became effective , they really started having some times , believe me they did. And they (the non- Christian religions) were losing their followers because they were beginning to learn some new truths, you see ? So they said, "Now wait a minute. Out in the courtyard are our gods Baal and Baalam. They are known as l ords and they are known as gods . So it is mandatory that you Christians call your Yahveh and your Elohim, lords and gods . Let's put this on an even basis! "

And so, under coercion and under force they did this very thing and you all know that it has led us into about 1200 or 1300 years of the DARK AGES or the APOSTASY because they had lost the name of the Father and his family . Those names have been substituted for , and the effects of the original words have been very definitely MISSING.

The words mean exactly what they say, and they carry a vibrant power that attracts the substance of faith , and you shall see proof of this before this day is over. The words "God" and "Yahveh" have been misused more than 10,000 times and under 10,000 titles in the Bible , and it is next to impossible to instruct people in the true name and even more difficult to get them to use it. That is , except you people and sometimes YOU still talk about the " Lord" don't you ? Which Lord are you talking about ? You say, well there's only one . Oh no there isn't . England is full of them. England is full of Lords ! So there are many Lords . But when you want to contact the Father , you're not going to get Him by tuning into some Lord .

You might get some information. A Lord might give you information. He might say, " Thus sayeth the Lord" . He might not even identify himself as to which Lord is speaking , but if you want things from headquarters , It'll be under the name the title of YAHVEH . All of it is INFORMATION, but all of it is not the same information .

It is difficult to UNLEARN a person. To empty their mind of preconceived errors is next to impossible . But it must be done if people are ever to know the truth. Our saviour said, "Verily I say unto you, except you become converted and become as little children, you shall not enter into the kingdom of heaven" . -- Matthew 18:3. This brings us into something that we have not possibly known before, and yet it's really so simple . It's really a very simple little thing . You will find that a little child does things that we do not do. A little child does some things naturally that we do not do at all , and we are going to have to learn to do them in order to come into the fullness of all that Yahveh has for us. How many have watched a tiny little baby when they breathe? You say, "Be careful now, when you touch the baby's head because it's very tender there. " And you watch a little baby that is breathing and the skull is gently separating , isn't that true ?

You'll find that the skull is separated into seven different parts , and they fit together real jagged if you've ever looked at a skull . The ones that the doctors keep in their office have to be glued because they are not normally one piece , but they are fit together very intricately by many jagged little surfaces but they go together just right .

Now, when a little child is asleep -- and they sleep about 20 out of 24 hours -- they breathe through their nose and they breathe very carefully . And when they do, this skull begins to separate. It goes back and forth and it moves freely , because it's designed to do just that thing . They do not breathe through their mouth, but they breathe through their nose, and there is a separation of the electrical forces . You are positive (+) on the right side and negative (-) on the left side, and if you don't think so, feel the right side of your face now and see if it isn't fairly coarse. Feel that. All right , now over on the left side feel how smooth it is . Because you are positive and negative, you also breathe and take the infinite light lines into your system, positive on the right side and negative on the left , and that's what gives the LIGHT to you.

And that is where the LIGHT is divided into your very being so that you can come to all of the knowledge by the spirit or the breath that is given to you. But we get lazy and we don't breathe deeply enough. We've just kind of found a place where we can idle. We're a high - speed instrument just learning to idle , you see? And when we learn to idle and take the path of least resistance , then our old skull comes together and over a period of years it becomes very tight . Then when we breathe, it is so tight that it doesn't separate at all -- but all the time, on the inside of the skull -- we're growing. So we hear something someday, and it strikes an arc of truth within us, and we decide that we're going to have to know more about this truth. There is something about this we must learn.

And it builds up inside of you, so you get hold of everything that you can read, you go to all kinds of New- Age lectures, you meet people who have had contacts, you dig into the scriptures -- maybe for the first time in all your life -- you read the Masters of the Far East, and all kinds of books. It might be any of these things . And all of it is helping , and you say, "My, I just can't seem to get these things through my head -- it gives me a HEADACHE . I feel such a tight band around my head when I study that I have to quit . I can only study so long ! " How many here have been through this ?

You will find, that as you come into a spiritual knowledge , something is trying to take place that you have caused a physical handicap to. And that is this. The Pituitary body, which lies just below the four lobes of your brain, has what is known as the "Turkish Saddle" (Sella Tursica) . We're going to look down on top of a skull or cranium. Now this isn't an egg I am picturing here... it's supposed to be the top of a head. Down inside is a tiny cradle of bone, the Turkish Saddle. Lying in this cradle is the Pituitary .

This Pituitary gland lies in this cradle of bone located in about the middle of your skull , and it has a couple of little bone wings coming out. Directly below this cradle is a little string coming down with a little object about the size of a pea. It's shaped like a little PINE CONE. It is known, not as a " PEEneal gland " but as a "Pineal gland" because it's like a PINE CONE, you see, and it's firmly attached by a very small muscle.

Now you have read, in the scriptures , that many times people have desired to die in later times, but their " worm would not turn" . This is the worm that it is speaking of, this Pituitary gland . Because when you are ill , or sick, it is forced out of its cradled position (lengthwise) and turns down crosswise in its Saddle. That shuts the switch off and you evacuate the body. It cuts your silver cord and you're gone , see?

On the other hand, when you come into a spiritual knowledge and understanding , you are made aware of things you never knew before. Put your hand on the top of your head right now and you'll find that you've got a bump coming up there. Do you find this ? It is raising up, and if you would check it by temperature you would find that it is 5 degrees warmer than any other part of the body .

Why ? Because it's under pressure. Why is it under pressure? Because it (the Pituitary) is trying to turn back to its normal position , which is lengthwise in the bone cradle in a left to right position rather than from the front to the back of the skull . In the average person, the Pituitary is cramped and twisting . However, if this condition is corrected, and the Pituitary is given plenty of space in which to function, then it can make a perfect contact with the Pineal gland . The electrical arc between these glands is intensified and your third eye begins to open, which is your inner vision . When you have this working you can close your natural eyes and think of anyone -- I don't care who they are or where they are -- and you will instantly see them . You will see where they are and what they are doing .

How can this be accomplished ? Just exactly like it speaks in the scripture, that when you come to the knowledge of these things you must come as a little child, otherwise down here you cannot enter the kingdom up there you see ? Because down here with this in operation you can close your eyes and literally SEE everything that is going on the kingdom of heaven right now. How can this be done ? A little child by breathing separates the cranial bones and relieves all the pressure so that this gland (Pituitary) can rise out of the cradle . And they don't have such a knot at the top of their head because the pressure has been eliminated.

You can take your skull (or have someone else do it) and flex these head bones and practice breathing very deeply through your nose, and literally break these tight sutures loose, so that when you breathe, your skull is going to breathe right along with you. And then when you feel caught up in this ecstatic position spiritually , you can close your eyes. And you're already spiritual enough that it'll turn your light on. And you will have the entrance into the heavenly knowledge by SIGHT. This is SPIRITUAL TELEVISION in perfection . This is one reason why you have to come as a little child and why you have to unlearn so many things that you have learned.

You say that you have been converted. But I ask you, are you willing to become converted as a little child ? Are you willing to become humble and knowing nothing in order to understand truth? You're going to have to put away all of the old dogmas and concepts that have been pounded into you, in order to understand this NEW AGE truth. And that's exactly what it is , because it has nothing to do with " religion " at all . Religion is something that man has made, but this is something that God made from the beginning, but you've forgotten about. And we're just UNLOCKING it again so that you can come into the knowledge that it's for YOU and you can have it again .

Now lay aside your old ideas and your preconceived ideas and open your mind and your heart, to the truth concerning our Father. We find in the scripture this passage, "What is His NAME and what is His son's NAME, if thou canst tell ? " -- Proverbs 30th chapter and 4th verse . Can you answer that question ?

You will remember that the Saviour in his last prayer before his crucifixion prayed saying , "I have manifested Thy name unto the men which Thou gavest me out of the world" -- John 17: 6. "Holy Father, keep through Thine own name those whom Thou has given me, that they may be one as we are. While I was with them in the world I kept them in Thy name.

Well , you mean the Master used the name of YAHVEH when he was on earth? Yes. That's the only way he was able to keep his followers, and keep them in their protection -- not by his name, no, but by the name of the Father. And it says so in John , the 17th chapter , verses 11 & 12.

Now the TRUE NAME is surely very important. The Saviour used these words in his closing prayer: "Oh righteous Father, the world has not known Thee, but I have known Thee. And these have known that Thou hast sent me, and I have declared unto them Thy name, and will declare it, that the love wherewith Thou hast loved me, may be in them and I in them. " And so it is through the knowledge of this secret name of God that this love is in you, according to John 17: 25-26.

This name YAHVEH , will bring the Father's love into you because it is of that vibratory frequency and when you sound that name within you it brings that love because it is that thing .

It is my purpose to declare unto you the NAME. Yet I am not sure that it is the Father's divine will and purpose to have all men everywhere to know His name. I don't believe that. The name is only to be known by His own people , those whom He has chosen out of this world. You were not chosen here. You were chosen somewhere else which is OUT of this world because you're only strangers and pilgrims here. The name is only to be known by His own people , those whom He has chosen out of this world, and those were not chosen on this world, according to John 15:16. John says that they were chosen before the world was. So if you were chosen before the world was, you couldn't have been chosen down here, could you ? No, you were chosen in ANOTHER PLACE . And you are the ones that the Master is speaking about: "I have chosen them out of this world, and I have given them back the Father's name. " And I'll tell you something. It is this... that the brothers upstairs are very anxious for His people -- the Father's people and His family here -- to get this name back, because they want them to start finding out WHO they are and get their sleeves rolled up and get ready to go to work.

Many of you are going to do what is known as the "greater works" . How many people here, by speaking the name of Yahveh, have seen their physical body come into balance -- that quick ! (hands raised) Quite a few.

All right , for those who haven't, touch your hands together . You notice that each one of your hands has a line right underneath the palm -- each one. Put those lines exactly together . Put your hands together . If you have not been balanced, chances are you'll now find that one hand is longer than the other one. All right , now separate your hands and separate your feet so we don't have any "short- circuit" there, and repeat after me:

> "Yahveh, in the name of Yahshua,
> I command electrons to balance me. "

Now measure your hands. They should be exactly the same length. In Independence , Missouri , the night before our scheduled lecture there, we went into the home of the one who was sponsoring this lecture . He had a group of people around and he said, "What can you tell us ? " We didn't know him, nor any of the folks that were there. We just came in off a long trip . We'd driven all the way from Oklahoma City , practically through a snow and ice storm, to get there. We came in about 7:00 O'clock in the evening and met the people for the first time, and they said, "We knew that you were coming . Now that you're here, we want you to speak to these people. " I said, "All right. "

So we talked a little bit about everything , and I decided to teach them about the power of this law of the Father in straightening physical bodies. So instead of straightening everybody all at once, we straightened them one at a time. There was an older lady sitting on the divan, and she was smiling very sweetly and gently . So we asked her, "Do you mind if we measure you ?" She replied , "I don't mind at all . " So I measured her hands and she was nearly one inch shorter on one side than the other. She was off nearly one inch. So I spoke the word and measured her again and she was perfect .

She said, "You know, I have my shoe built up about 7/8ths of an inch. " I replied , "Can you take the build- up out ?" She looked at everyone else and then said, "Yes , I guess so. " She took this build-up out of her shoe and put her shoe back on. I said, "Now get up and walk around" . She looked at everyone and they looked at her, and I thought "What's the matter here? " But she got up and walked around. I said, "Does that feel all right ?" "It feels wonderful, just wonderful! " So I went on about the lecture.

A month later we'd had a series of lectures at the Palmer House in Chicago , and we returned by that way and this lady said, "I'm working now!" "You are?" , I replied , "Where ?" "At the Unity farm at Lee's Summit, Missouri. I have something to do with the ministry of children. "

"That's fine . " I said.

"I want you and your wife to have dinner with me out there and meet the head of Unity . "

I said, "Yes , I'll be glad to do that. " So we did. We went out and met the head of Unity organization , and had lunch with them. We had a grand time, a grand time. This lady personally walked us all over the farm, and we two were just about ready to fall , weren't we Tarna , and at the end of the day this elderly lady was still going strong. And she said, "By the way, I don't know if I or anyone else ever told you or not, but before you spoke the word for me that night, I had been an invalid for 15 years.

That's why everyone was looking at everyone else when she got up and started walking around.

There was a little girl who came to our meetings in Iowa. She was about 11 or 12 years old, and she said, "Oh, I enjoy these things . I just love to know what goes on up in the sky . But I sat on the wrong side of the auditorium and I couldn't hear what you were saying . " I asked her, "What is wrong ?" The aunt that had brought the little girl to the meeting said, "Well , she has no ear drum on the right side. "

I said, "Is that so?" I placed my finger in her right ear and said, "Yahveh, in the name of Yahshua, design a place for an eardrum for this little girl and put it there. " And I held my finger tight in her ear and whispered in the ear that didn't have an eardrum and she answered every question I asked. She said, "I can hear as good out of this ear now as I can out of the other ear. " "That fine, " I said, "thank you very much! "

These things really happened. It is not anything that I can do that you cannot do, because every one of you can do these things when you are in tune with the secret name of God. It is being delivered back into your hands as part of your inheritance, like a long - lost treasure of Light . Here we may ask the question, how and why was this true name LOST through history ? Haven't you often wondered why we haven't known it all the time ? What caused us to LOSE this very, very precious knowledge and power?

The answer is that the 10 tribes of Israel were dispersed throughout the world in 721 B.C. Ten of the tribes were scattered. They became blinded to their identity and lost their mother language which was Hebrew. But let me say in passing that they will not be lost or blinded forever, these people . And here is the scripture : "For lo, I will command. And I will sift the House of Israel among all nations like as corn is sifted in a sieve, yet shall not the least grain fall upon the earth. " Amos, Chapter 9, verse 9. "

For I would not, brethren, that you should be ignorant of this mystery, " says Paul, "lest you should be wise in your own conceits and blindness as it happened to Israel until the fullness of the gentiles be come in, and so all Israel shall be saved. " How much of Israel ? ALL Israel . Don't let anybody kid you now, because the scriptures cannot be broken says Yahshua. " There shall come out of ZION the deliverer who shall turn away ungodliness from Jacob , for this is my covenant unto them, when I shall take away their sins . " -- Romans 11:25-27 .

We know that we are living in the LAST DAYS . Why do we say, " Last days " ? We say it because we're coming to the end of the element that is known as TIME[8] . When we come back onto course with infinite light , that TIME BARRIER is going to lay down and the past-time barrier is going to lay down and there'll be no beginning and no ending . And there'll be no clocks. We just won't be interested in clocks or calendars or such. We are in the " Last Days " and the time has come for the blindness to be wiped out of the eyes of every Israelite , and their identity made known and the truth restored . And by the word "ISRAELITE " we do not mean the people who are presently inhabiting the nation of Israeli .

In 585 B.C. , the tribes of Judah and Benjamin were carried captive into Babylon . Seventy years later a few of them under Esra and Neamiah returned to Palestine. But for the most part, they were terribly mixed with the heathen. Oh yes. They were terribly mixed with the heathen both by blood and by language . This is the scripture : " Their children spoke half the speech of Ashdod, and could not speak in the language of Judah, (Hebrew) but according to the language of each people . 11 When they were carried away about the next generation , they were losing sight of the secret name of God, and all of the Hebrew language .

And I might tell you and it might be interesting to you to know, that many people who claim to be Jews or of Judah, speak what is known as Yiddish. Only 30% of the Yiddish language is derived from Hebrew. But 72% of the ENGLISH language is derived from Hebrew -- 72%!

At this time that they began to lose their language , it was then that the Old Testament scriptures were rewritten, probably by Esra . And the title " Lord" was substituted for YAHVEH , and the title "God" was substituted for ELOHIM. That took all recognition of who the Father and His family were, out of the understanding of all the people . They did not even remember that they were of ISRAEL . The word ISRAEL does NOT mean a nation which is not even named Israel (the earthly nation is called "ISRAELI ") , because there is no reigning king of Israel on this world. The reigning king of ISRAEL is in the heavenlies, you see.

This title Lord was transplanted into the hearts and minds of the people to cause them literally to FORGET their inheritance. Now this was due in part to fear . For they were afraid to speak the true name above a whisper , even up to this day . And

---

8. TIME NO MORE, an important. Monograph by Michael X. Barton,

the ones who caused this name to be hidden are the unsuspected ones mentioned in Revelation 2:9 and Revelation 3:9, -- "Those that say they are jews and are not, but are of the Synagogue of Satan" . It says that those people even to this day will not speak this name. They are afraid it will destroy them , so instead of using the name Yahveh, they take the word Adonai.

They will not speak the name Yahveh even in their consciousness , or audibly above a whisper . And in all their special services where they are required to use the true name, they substitute for it the Phoenician title of Adonai, which is equivalent to the titles God or Lord. That is what it signifies: Lord, Tetragrammaton , YHVH. It is a false title.

Webster's New Twentieth Century Dictionary gives the following definition, quote: JEHOVAH which is a noun, and the modern translation of Hebrew, the sacred name of God, the so-called Tetragrammaton YHVH. The vowels appear through arbitrary transference of vowel points of the word ADONAI, meaning "my lord" , "God" , "The Lord". End quote.

Now the arbitrary transference of the vowel points of the Phoenician word Adonai has rendered the name in English : JEHOVAH , because it was not taken from the Tetragrammaton but is taken from the false word that was used in place of the true one. Jehovah is a word of three syllables , and actually it is not a word but it is a SENTENCE. JE means "past" . HO means "present " . VAH means "future" . Past, Present and Future is the meaning of the word JEHOVAH , thereby making it a sentence. When written in full it means the past, present and the future One.

This is a good definition of Yahshua the Messiah, according to Hebrews 13:8 where it says that he is the same yesterday , today and forever ... our (king invisible , immortal in the heavens. But the true name of the Father 7 is YAHVEH , which is both a name and a sentence, and this is true of nearly all Hebrew names. As examples , the name Yahshua which is the name of our saviour, means "Yahveh is salvation" . The very meaning of his name shows that He, the Father, is the saviour . The meaning of the word Jehosaphant is "Yahveh hath judged " . The word Jehoshua means "Yahveh is strong" . Nearly all Hebrew nouns, the names of persons, places and things are contractions of Yahveh or Elohim. For instance, the name ISRAEL means "a prince with Elohim" . And a prince is always next to a king , isn't that so? Israel means a prince with Elohim.

The word Ezekiel means "Elohim is strong" . It means that the family of Yahveh is strong. That is the meaning of the word Ezekiel . Every word of the Bible has a wonderful meaning and not a word is wasted.

What did the king say that he came for ? Well , first of all , Israel was scattered. Ten tribes were scattered in 721 B.C. and 2-1 /2 tribes in the year 521 B.C. The exile kings of Israel had no authority whatsoever , and the children were rapidly forgetting who they were. So the king , immortal, invisible , eternal of the heavens literally came down here to do one thing .

I've asked many preachers who Yahshua came to seek and to save. They tell me invariably the same answer every time: "Oh brother, those who were lost. " The fact is , he did not say any such thing . Here is the scripture: "I am not sent but unto the lost sheep of the House of Israel . " The Master says this in his own words in Matthew 15:24.

The New Testament is written to and for the 12 tribes which are scattered abroad, it says in James the first chapter and the first verse. It is not written to the heathen. It is not written to those who would follow Buddha and Zoroaster . It is to the 12 tribes of ISRAEL who are scattered abroad.

Every patriarch and every prophet and every king and every apostle , every disciple and every priest and every judge was an ISRAELITE . Every one of them. You also -- speaking of you as "lively stones" -- are built up a spiritual house and holy priesthood to offer spiritual sacrifices acceptable to God. But you are a chosen generation and a royal priesthood . You are a nation, and the only nation that He recognizes because you are of the nation of the KINGDOM OF HEAVEN that is being established upon the surface of this world . And.... you are a PECULIAR people !

Believe in flying saucers ? You must be peculiar ! A peculiar people -- that you should show forth the praises of Him who hath called you out of darkness. Out of darkness? Certainly , because you didn't know who you were . But you're beginning to see the light . He has called you out of darkness into His marvelous light , so that you are no longer scattered, but are now a people of God or the ELOHIM . And you have obtained mercy because once again you know the secret name of the Father .

CHAPTER 7
Upon a White Stone Written
◆

"I will give you the hidden manna to eat and will give him (who overcometh) a WHITE STONE. " The Holy Scripture says this. Now the White Stone is that Christ which is in you. And the reason why it is named a stone is because it is a portion of building material. It had to be given to us according to that which we would understand. We've always known that the temple that the Kingdom would be made out of had to be built out of something that is substantial. And we know, пут that of all the things we've ever seen that have been built and have lasted hundreds of years and sometimes even thousands of years , that they have been built out of STONE . Isn't that true ? YOU

This Stone is filled with Light . And it is a WHITE stone, and in the Stone a NEW NAME is written. That Stone is the Christ consciousness within you , and it is within you that the name is written. We haven't USED that name, but it's written there nonetheless -- "Which no man knoweth save he that receiveth it . " Well , if you don't have that Stone in there you'll never know what's written on it , because it has to be revealed on the inside.

I'll tell you, it's like a story I once heard which is so practical and it fits this situation perfectly . There was a man who was blind. His name was Elmer. And his friend said, "Elmer, I'm going to have my friend explain something to you. " Elmer said, "Oh, that will be fine! I'm glad ! "

So the man's friend walks in and the man said to him, " Friend , Elmer over here is blind and I'm trying to give him a little education. Here is a white ball. I want you to take this white ball over to Elmer and explain it to him. Now you know Elmer . He will probably recognize you by your voice. Elmer has been blind since birth. Naturally he has never seen a white ball. But I want you to take this white ball and explain it to him."

So the friend walks over to Elmer and says, "Elmer . " "Yes, I recognize your voice, you're my old friend. " " Yes, that's right . Glad to see you, Elmer . I want to explain something to you because we want to give you a little education. Elmer , hold out your hand."

So Elmer holds out his hand. "Elmer, this is a white ball. " Elmer takes the ball and says, "It's round. Does that make it white ? " The friend answers, "No, it's round and that causes you to know its SHAPE. That which you feel as round is the shape of the ball . " So Elmer squeezes the ball and says, "It's soft. Does that make it white ? " "No, Elmer, being soft is the composition of the ball . But being soft does not make the ball white. " So Elmer smells the ball and notices that it has a peculiar odor, and he says, "Is that a white odor ?" "No, you cannot smell white. That happens to be the vibration or the odor that's emanating from this ball . "

Elmer takes a bite of it. "Oh, " he says, "this tastes awful. Is that a white taste ? " "No, you can't taste white. " So no matter how the friend of Elmer tried to explain to him what a white ball was , he could tell the shape of the ball , he could tell the composition of the ball , he could tell the smell of the ball , he could tell the taste of the ball or he could bounce the ball and get the sound of the bounce, but he COULD NOT KNOW what a white ball was because he had no VISION on the outside .

The same thing holds true about the WHITE STONE that is within you, because it is beyond the range of your mortal vision . Things which are seen are temporary. And this stone is that Christ within you which has a NEW NAME written on it , which is on an eternal plane . And the fact that it is on an eternal plane and dwells within you, it is out of the range of your vision. Yet it is written that this name is written on that White Stone. If this is so, then how in the world are you supposed to read it ?

The only way that you can read it , ladies and gentlemen , is by the spiritual INNER vision because that is the only way that it can be seen and you have to have eyes to see. In other words , it has to be revealed from the inside. The only way that Elmer could know that the ball was white is for it to be revealed to Elmer on the INSIDE as to what WHITE is , because he could not tell . He had no facilities on the outside to tell . It had to be revealed to him on the inside, and this White Stone that you will receive , with your NEW NAME written on it, is written on this White Stone within. And the Kingdom of Heaven is where ? WITHIN you.

And with these stones that have this new name written thereon, that are within you and you and you, the Master said, "I will build my kingdom " . They are LIVELY stones. They're not dead, they're not tired . They never get tired. They are that urgency that you feel to be of service to all mankind. They are that love that you feel for people who might be altogether UNlovely . They are that kindred feeling that you feel that draws you to nice people , and you like to be around them.

They have an exact place . Because this kingdom is going to build into a tremendous body. And each one of these stones fit in a certain way in a certain place , you see. And without all the stones the kingdom cannot be completed . You couldn't take a stone out from here and one from there. ALL of those stones have to be there. And all of those stones have this new name written on them, and that is of the substance of THAT stone of the originating place of that stone.

And finally when the outer man begins to let go and the INNER MAN begins to stand up and he begins to put his hands in your hands and his feet in your feet, then he is going to discover many things . Oh yes . As he begins to stand up and look around, he begins to HEAR and he begins to SEE . And when he does, you're going to find out what family you belong to and what importance you play in all of the universes.

"He that overcometh, the same shall be clothed in white raiment. " It says this in Revelation 3:5. And what is this white raiment going to be? Man is the only creature on the face of the world, on the earth or in the earth or any place out of this earth that we've ever been able to see, that has to wear ARTIFICIAL CLOTHES . The birds have clothes. We have a cat and a dog, they have clothing . They never have to worry about getting a new fur coat every winter because they get one. They are clothed upon. And who does it ? The Father takes care of them. The Bible says He even takes care of the little sparrows.

We're going to find that we don't need artificial clothing one of these days , because we're going to be clothed upon with WHITE RAIMENT . And that is going to be spun with Infinite Light intelligence . It is going to be inpenetrable. I mean it will be the best bullet- proof vest that anybody in this world ever heard about, because it cannot be penetrated . It will be worn by those in the time spoken of by Joel , when he says, they shall fall on a sword and the wound of the foe shall not cause blood to flow. They can fall on a sword and they're not going to be injured because nothing can penetrate that light -force. This white raiment is impenetrable .

And we're coming up to the time NOW where we are finally coming into the knowledge of the FULLNESS and the stature of the perfect man in CHRIST (which is this anointing) and when we do then we're going to put on this clothing , this white raiment to where it wouldn't surprise me if someday soon you could go to your wardrobe and pitch it all out, because you're going to have better clothing . I mean this literally and honestly , right now. This is something you are due to experience .

"He that overcometh, <u>shall be clothed in White Raiment</u>, and I will not blot out his name in the Book of Life , but I will confess his name before the Father and before His angels . " So the angels come into this play too. In other words, there are many people in this world who would like to be working closely with the angels , with the Messengers of the Most High , and I'd just like to remind you people of one thing. When the word gets around that you -- each one of you -- is coming into this knowledge , then, the Master said that he would confess your name before the angels .

You Are Going to Work With Angels

They (the angels or spacemen) are going to say, "Well now, there is someone that we can use. I think I'll just pay him (or her) a visit . There is someone who is coming into a place that they can be of SERVICE to all mankind. I think that I'll go down and form a working alliance with them, and put them to work right along with us."

It says that you're going to work with angels . Yes it does. And it says that many people will see these angels coming to their very door, but they are not going to recognize them unless them recognize them by -- a little buzzing sensation on the INSIDE . It says in your bible that a stranger will come to your door and be careful that you don't offend him " lest you entertain an angel unawares" . Doesn't it say that ? So this space program has been set in order a long time ago. Angels are coming to this world now, and to other worlds . Oh yes , many of the other planets of our solar system have to have help because they're OUT OF COURSE with infinite light too.

All things that are visible to this physical vision are out of course. Oh, they're closer in than we. But they are also relying on higher sources for help . You're going to have an opportunity to answer the door one of these days and you're going to be facing someone who is beautiful to behold. And you're going to be able to offer yourself into service .

We've known for a long time that when you come fully into this service , and when you come fully to a place of awakening , then you're going to have a ministry -- oh yes that is not just going to cover this world, but it is going to cover WORLDS... WORLDS. We've been told that by different sources and directly . I think that's wonderful beyond my comprehension . Do you know why ? Because I'm not ready

71

for it . But it gives me a challenge , you see. And it gives YOU a challenge for all of us to work together as a unit in a family , to know who we are , to RAISE that consciousness so we will be valued in a place of real service.

Now I'm going to read of Revelation 3:8 & 12. It says, "I know thy works. Behold, I have set before thee an open door" . After you've come into this knowledge and after you find out that you have that STONE which is that "essential Christ " within you, which is the stone that is to be used in building the kingdom which shall come "without observation " ; and when you come to the knowledge that you are the same substance as the vine and the life of the vine , when you come to all of this knowledge and you begin to feel like you're all a closeknit part of a FAMILY that is of the same nationality which is HEAVENLY in source, then he says, "I have set before thee an open door" .

Now the Master said, "I am the way I am the door" , and if you are of the same substance as that door itself , then you can walk through that door because you're on the same vibratory level . You can see the door if you're made out of the same vibratory substance. "Behold, I have set before thee an open door , and no man can shut it" . Oh, there's going to be a lot of men try to close a lot of doors during this END- TIME period . But I mean that the people of the NEW AGE are coming into a knowledge and an understanding that has not been known since the beginning of time . The beginning of TIME was the beginning of TROUBLE , because Time is not in the frequency of eternity .

"For thou hast a little strength , " How many have a little strength ? How many feel that it's an awful little strength ? O.K. "And hast kept My word" , What is the word ? The word is YAHVEH. Now, the preachers will tell you that the "word" is the Bible. They'll say, "Brother, that's the word" . Oh no. They were talking about the WORD before they HAD a bible. They were talking about the word that was the substance of all the things that we can possibly hope for , which is "YAHVEH " (YHVH) . "And which has not denied My name.

"And I will write upon him the name of My Elohim, and of the City of My Elohim (that's the Heavenly City) . That's just one of the heavenly cities but we're concerned now with this planet . The other planets have the same type of a heavenly city , the New Jerusalem , which cometh down out of heaven "from My Elohim" . The "Family " is in charge of it now, you see. There are 12,000 of each of the twelve tribes that went up there when the Master did, and they've taken charge of building and making this place , "Whose builder and maker is Elohim" , and they're renovating it and getting it ready to come back here. "I will write upon

72

him My New Name. "

How plain can it be, ladies and gentlemen , that He's going to write upon you this NEW NAME , that He's going to give you a WHITE STONE with this name written upon it ? It's going to be in the stone first , in the Christ within your heart. And then you're going to come to the knowledge of it and it will become a SEAL in your forehead. The divine SEAL is the name YAHVEH. That is so important to you. It is so very, very important .

He said, "I will give you a new name" , didn't he say that ? And it will be upon a WHITE STONE, which is YOU. "I will write upon it a new name which no man will know (unless you want to reveal it) and this name shall be better than that of sons and daughters . It will be better, because you're going to be known by your Cosmic Name which is the name of the planetary prince (or princess) which was ordained by the Order of Melchizedek from the very beginning .

Now we do have secret agents of that royal priesthood on the surface of this world today , yet we do not see the kingdom of heaven around us. But we have been told that with the coming of the Master that it was at hand. Let's look into this a little bit. The kingdom of God is most surely , most certainly , a secret, invisible (because it's eternal) empire that is known only to the initiated. I mean by the "initiated" those who know that it exists and WHERE it is , and who have had their consciousness raised so that they can SEE it. They have been called, and chosen. Then, after being called and chosen they are FAITHFUL . It is necessary that you be faithful to what you have been called and chosen to.

In the Sermon on the Mountain Jesus said, " Blessed are the poor in spirit , for theirs is the kingdom of heaven. And blessed are they who are persecuted for righteousness ' sake, for theirs is the kingdom of heaven . Whosoever , therefore, shall break one of the commandments and shall teach men so, he shall be called the least in the kingdom of heaven. But whosoever shall do and teach them, the same shall be called great in the kingdom of heaven for I say to you that except your righteousness (your balance in infinite light) shall exceed the righteousness of the scribes and the pharisees , you shall in no case enter into the kingdom of heaven. "

He is telling you that you have to come into the balance where you vibrations are raised, or you cannot even SEE it, for that's where it is. And we've been telling you that the time is coming when we're changing from the 3rd density to the 4th, that you're going to be QUICKENED in your mortal body. Then the things which are solid here in 3-D, that is houses, and land, and cattle and dogs and cats and all things that you normally see with your physical vision , are going to be seen through . And suddenly you'll find that you're in a wonderful place , and you'll even understand the song of the birds . Why ? Because you've been quickened to understand the song all the way through . It's going to be wonderful!

Last night and nearly all night long , it seems I was someplace and I don't remember this morning where it was, but I was someplace . And my desire that was being made known was this : that you people , not some other people someplace else in the world , but you people would take these things to heart and understand them, that your understanding might be quickened . That all of this message might go all over the world, all over the world, and that you might be the one to take it .

CHAPTER 8
The Melchizedek Order

During the time of Abraham there was a person on the surface of this world by the name of Melchizedek , who was the King of Salem which means the King of Peace. The Melchizedek priesthood is the priesthood between man -- the natural man on the planets -- and their Father ; and Melchizedek is half- way in between to make the connection once again . When this thing comes on course physically it must come back on course SPIRITUALLY also, and he is the one who is going to draw the two together.

The angels of God, your brothers and sisters up above, and the brothers and sisters down below, are going to be drawn together and placed even as one family , because it is written that we shall ALL come to the unity of the faith. And faith is that substance of things hoped for which will last forever, which is an eternal thing . It is everlasting .

Certainly the world is divided now. We are divided into all kinds of nations, we are divided into all kinds of "notions" , we are divided into all kinds of political systems and into all kinds of religious denominations ! But believe me, that when he says we should all come to the unity of the faith, he meant the Presbyterians , the Mormons, the Catholics , the Buddhists, the Confucianists, the Mohammedans, he meant the whole business. They shall all come to the unity of the faith in the fullest meaning of that word.

The Master has set forth this ministry for bringing all people together to find out first who all people are . Then they want the people to know after they are chosen into this Order of Melchizedek for bringing all things together -- that all things are possible . But in order to know that all things are possible , they have to first find out what all things are. And he has stated that the time will come when he will REVEAL UNTO YOU ALL THINGS. That's a lot of things , isn't it ? But if you have found the beginning you've found the ending, and if you've found the ending you've found the beginning ; because it's a Great Circle of Eternity without end.

It's like following around a solid ring . You cannot find the beginning nor the ending of it . When the time comes that you stand up and say, "I am the Alpha and Omega -- the beginning and the ending" , then you will start to come into a consciousness that the Melchizedek priesthood is everlasting, without beginning of days nor ending of years . Without descent, because you have always been. You are after the order of Melchizedek when you have come into the knowledge of the spiritual heritage that is yours.

When Adam left the Garden of Eden, he didn't leave empty- handed. He carried with him 5 emblems. It is important for you to know this because it is a vital part of the real Melchizedek story . The names of these five emblems and what they were is as follows:

The first was a Sapphire Cane. This was taken out of the Garden of Eden. Second, were the Holy Garments. Third, was Gold. If you've ever wondered where the "Gold of Ophirr " came from, this is it. This Gold is found in the lost Garden of Eden. Fourth, is Frankincense, and the fifth is Myrrh . The story of how these emblems were lost and found is very interesting , and also they have an important bearing on the history of man.

Before the transgression and all the time that Adam and Eve were in the Garden of Eden they were clothed with beautiful white garments of heavenly light , according to the scriptures . Yahveh, who is our Father, gave to every animal its own natural clothing . All animals are born clothed, but to Adam and Eve who were His own children , He had not given a natural clothing . They were clothed with heavenly robes of light , it says in Genesis. But when they transgressed , that is , changed over from a total reliance in full faith upon Yahveh, to a greater reliance upon personal self will , they were stripped of their garments of light . And then they discovered that they were naked.

You now have to wear an artificial clothing , but when you come into the balance of this substance of faith which is infinite light , you will be clothed upon by LIGHT itself , and I think that's pretty wonderful, don't you ?

We are told to put on the armour of light , in Romans 13:12. And it says "Put ye on Yahveh-Yahshua the Messiah, " in Romans 13:14. Now remember that when we are speaking of the "Messiah " we are speaking of the Christ within us. "Christ " means "the anointed one", and Messiah in the Hebrew means "the anointed one" . And in the Greek, "Christos " also means "the anointed one" . So, when you put on the anointing , you have put on the Messiah, according to the scriptures . And again we read, " Put on the whole armour of Yahveh" , in Ephesians 6:11. And " Put on the new man, which after Yahveh, is created in righteousness and true holiness". Ephesians 4:24. When you are anointed you put on garments of LIGHT .

I'm building up to something , because today we're speaking about the Great White Brotherhood, and the Order of Melchizedek or the Melchizedek Priesthood. And right here I'd like to call your attention to the secret significance of a symbol that is most important to you , and that is the symbol of "sheep" . The Sheep symbol is far greater than most people realize . A sheep is the symbol of the family of Yahveh, His fore- ordained and predestinated sons and daughters who pre- existed before the world was made, and who have since then at intervals been incarnated in the flesh in the family of Adam, are identified as " sheep".

All of the natural, earthly races of men hated a sheep . The Egyptians would not eat mutton, and they would not sit by a tallow candle light , and they would not wear woolen clothing . When Jacob and his family were brought by Joseph to Egypt , the Egyptians did not know that this family consisted of shepherds . If they had known it , they would have never permitted them to enter into Egypt at all . As late as the days of Moses, 430 years after Jacob had gone down into Egypt , the Egyptians still had a bitter hatred of sheep . A sheep was symbolic of something that they were against .

If the Israelites had offered a sheep on an altar anywhere in Egypt , the Egyptians would have destroyed them. That was the SYMBOL of something that had been handed down and the very natural races of the Egyptians resented it intensely . They had no time for the symbol which Yahveh had set for His people , which were SHEEP . And if any Israelite had dared offer a sheep upon the altar in the sight of the Egyptians they would have been immediately executed. In all the 430 years that they were in Egypt , they never offered a sheep in the sacrifice until the Passover -- the night before they left Egypt . That's the very first time, according to the Bible. They pretended to be cattle- herders. This was to keep the Egyptians from knowing that they were members of the Great White Brotherhood.

Listen to this , because you're in it. And up till now you haven't known it. The sheep symbol is an important thing for you to remember, because sheep (Yahveh's family) have a direct bearing upon your life and upon your life's ministry because you are a member of the Great White Brotherhood and this is something that you don't join . You're either in it or you are NOT in it. And if you are in it you were born in it , and you were born in it by your Heavenly Father Yahveh and your Heavenly Mother Kahveh.

We are talking about some of the EMBLEMS that were brought out of the Garden of Eden by Adam, and how necessary it is to know the symbology of SHEEP in the

Bible . And we've come down to this point , that if the Israelites had offered a sheep anywhere on an altar in Egypt while they were in bondage, the Egyptians would have destroyed them. The Egyptians had hated sheep , and they would not attend anything by the light of the tallow candle, at all . They would not even wear woolen clothing , because they hated everything that a sheep stood for .

When you have a "New Birth " -- which is a "virgin birth" -- then you are born into the Great White Brotherhood, and it is a Brotherhood symbolized by SHEEP , and the most interesting part of this is going to be given to you just a little bit later here. Now, let's consider the other emblems.

The five emblems were handed down over a period of 1656 years from Adam to seth to Enos to Cainan to Mahalaleel to Jared (from whom came a branch which later on called themselves Mormons. The Latter - Day Saints came off this branch and settled in the North American country) to Methuselah to Enoch to Lamech and then to Noah.

I'll repeat what these 5 emblems were. The first was a Sapphire Cane, the second was the Holy Garments , the third was the Gold of Ophirr , the fourth was Frankincense, the fifth was Myrrh . It's important to know that these things were handed all the way down from Adam on down to Noah. Now, Adam and Noah and all of those inbetween who had held these Garments and all of the 5 emblems that had been handed down to that time , were all members of the Great White Brotherhood. And listen to this, each one ruled over a kingdom on earth before the flood and they were in constant contact with Yahveh Himself . And each one of these that received the emblems was a king . So there were ten kingdoms from Adam to Noah.

To find out the number of years each kingdom lasted , and which ones were parallel or contemporary, study carefully this scripture: Genesis 5: verses 1 through 32. It will give you a complete rundown on these kingdoms and the length of time that these kingdoms lasted and each one of them had as SYMBOLS the very emblems of the White Brotherhood that had been passed down all the way from Adam (and he got them from someone higher) .

Now, after the flood a very strange thing happened, and this may clear something up for you. Noah became intoxicated, remember? Hedrank wine and became drunken and was uncovered within his tent, according to Genesis the 9th chapter , verses 20 & 21. Now Noah did not get drunk intentionally . It was NOT intentional, because before the flood the earth had been upright at the poles .

Remember, it was at the time of the flood that the world turned UPSIDE DOWN. There was no fermentation before the world turned upside down and became out of course, and Noah was used to drinking wine. It was very sweet to the taste and it was wonderful. And I think perhaps they drank more "fruit of the vine" then, than they drank of water, by far. But it was not a fermented grapejuice .

The energy of the moon before the flood was equal to that of the sun today , did you know that ? It was, according to Isaiah, the 30th chapter , 26th verse. There was no fermentation , no rust and no decay before the flood, none whatsoever -- incredible though this may seem to us today .

Noah did not know that the earth had turned upside down, according to Isaiah the 24th chapter , 1st verse. He didn't know this had happened. He knew that he had gone through a deluge of water and had been tossed upon a high sea. But he didn't even know where it came from, because it had been the vaporous canopy of water that now envelops Venus. That canopy consisted of the waters that had been divided from the waters -- the salt water (the + element) was divided from the fresh water (-) on this earth and when this earth turned upside down, the POLARITY was changed. And for 40 days and 40 nights that vaporous canopy came down upon the surface of this world and caused the oceans that you have now.

He didn't know that "all the foundations" of the earth were out of course, that it had moved completely out of course with infinite light , according to Psalms 82:5. He did not know that the moon had become a dead planet , and that the energy of the sun had been reduced to one- seventh of what it had been before the flood. He did not know that he was going to die like earthly men. But fermentation and rapid multiplication of bacteria , rust and decay had set in, and he drank the highly fermented wine without knowing of its intoxicating power. He was naked in his tend, which was his own home, and he had laid aside the symbolic Garments.

This is important , because you've often wondered, if you're a member of the Great White Brotherhood, what happened to the reign of these kings which was in an unbroken lineage down to the time of Noah, why hasn't it continued ? Why has the present evil world system come in -- I mean the present world systems of fascism, communism, and all the other kinds of "isms" that are controlling the government in what is known as the "present evil world" ? Well, here is a scripture .

"And Ham, the father of Canaan, committed adultery with a concubine of Noah, when he unlawfully went into Noah's tent. He also stole the five emblems, including the holy symbolic garments . The curse was not pronounced upon Ham, but upon his sons. It said, "Cursed be Canaan, " in Genesis 9:25. Thus the Canaanites unlawfully got possession of the emblems and by usurped authority they completely controlled the world for more than 400 years , after the flood. Nimrod, who built Babylon , was their greatest king , and he ruled the world for a long time. They established many religions and multiplied , and manufactured great images and became worshippers of all the stars of heaven. They were star worshippers . The Canaanites developed into 31 nations and spread out over the earth.

The Great White Brotherhood did not begin to emerge from Canaanite control nor recover what they had lost until the time of the great patriarch Abraham . That was a long time. And the beginning of bloodshed was seen during that period of time . The physical upbuild and the customs of men and women were changed , because before the flood, no one ever slew an animal for anything to eat. But directly after the flood and after the control was wrenched out of the hands of the Great White Brotherhood they began to slaughter , and they began to eat flesh , and they began to do all these things that had not been permitted under the rule of the Great White Brotherhood .

So the chemical composition of the bodies began to change and it began to come " out of tune" as it were, because the body vibrations began to be lowered in frequency until they lost the sound of the guiding voice of the shepherd , and we FORGOT WHO WE WERE . We forgot that we were members of the Great White Brotherhood.

Yahveh called Abraham out of Ur, the city of the Chaldees, and Melchizedek himself met Abraham. Oh, what a powerful person -- Melchizedek ! He met Abraham, gave him bread and wine and blessed him. Now, the Melchizedek Order had operated secretly as " counter- spies " in all of the Canaanite nation, and had gotten possession of the 5 emblems again . They took them back. The Melchizedek Order literally went in and possessed what was their inheritance. They took back the 5 emblems which the Canaanites had stolen from Noah, and the priesthood of Melchizedek is the highest and holiest priesthood of Yahveh on earth.

It always operates secretly and never openly. It is not a human organization, neither can any man join it. Yahshua the Messiah calls and chooses those who are priests in this order . He also sustains them and guides them and they do not depend upon a human organization for their support. And in speaking of the Melchizedek Order I do not have in mind, nor am I affiliated with any organization or religion or any other lodge group that calls themselves by this name. This is a HERITAGE, and not something that has been formulated in the minds of men.

Those who Yahshua has called and chosen and sent into the Order of Melchizedek, know each other by the witness of the Holy Spirit. Spirit witnesses with spirit and our personalities do not clash, in any way. We LOVE each other. And when we meet we have a consciousness of always having known each other. I don't see a STRANGER in this place! I feel a kindred spirit. I feel a kindred spirit. If you cannot understand how that you feel a kindred spirit, then it's because you don't belong. Because if you belong to this thing, it is your heritage, and you will FEEL that thing when you are with these people. You will feel the witness of your spirit with their spirit, and confirmed by the Holy Ghost.

Melchizedek is only mentioned twice in the Old Testament. Once in Genesis the 14th chapter, verse 18 through 20. And again in the 110th Psalm which I shall quote and comment on. "The lord shall send the rod of thy strength out of Zion. Rule thou in the midst of thine enemies.", it says in Psalms 110:2. The Melchizedek Order does rule in spite of the fact that the enemies are right now in power. But the Melchizedek Order has the authority and the power because it was given to them of Yahveh to be the ones who are ruling, and the divine plan of Yahveh has not been destroyed. It is being carried out perfectly, just like he intended, right now.

"Thy people shall be willing in the day of thy power in the beauty of holiness, from the womb of the morning, thou hast the dew of YOUTH. The Lord has sworn and will not repent, thou art a priest forever after the order of Melchizedek." Psalms 110: 3 & 4.

This Melchizedek is the Christ that dwells within us. It is a King eternal that dwells within us. It is a King of peace. Not a prince of peace, but a King of peace. It is also a King of Love. It dwells as the Inner Man. It is the inner man that is renewed day by day. Oh, the flesh may deteriorate, but the inner man is renewed day by day and that is the Melchizedek priest-. hood, the Christ that is within you.

Now the following scripture tells us exactly WHO he is, and who the former Melchizedek was. He was YAHSHUA the Messiah. He was Yahshua in his pre-existence on the earth. And it is a wonderful truth for all those who are seeking truth: "For this Melchizedek, King of Salem, priest of the Most High God, who met Abraham returning from the slaughter of kings, and blessed him. To whom also, Abraham gave a tenth part of all. First being, by interpretation: King of

Righteousness , and after that also King of Salem which is the King of Peace. Without father and without mother, without descent, having neither beginning of days nor end of life , but made like unto the Son of God, abideth a priest continually . "

The 5 emblems were handed down all the way from Adam to Noah, then stolen by the Canaanites, then reclaimed by the counter- spies of the Melchizedek Order , and finally delivered back into the hands of Yahshua at the time of his birth in Bethlehem . These symbolic emblems were returned to Yahshua by the Wise Men (secret agents of Melchizedek) who brought him "presents " of Gold, Frankincense and Myrrh . It is thought that the Holy Garments were lambskin wrappings . And the GOLD was presented to Christ the King , because he was literally the King . He was not just a prince , not just a saviour, not just a lowly person as some churches would have you believe; but it was presented to him as a King of Kings .

The Sapphire Cane was kept by Joseph , the Frankincense and the Myrrh was kept by his uncle, Joseph of Arimathea, and by Nicodemus and by a woman by the name of Mary . They were the keepers of these emblems. All of whom were members of the Great White Brotherhood, and secret agents of the Order of Melchizedek. Such is the true story of Melchizedek as it is known by the brothers upstairs , and by his true followers here .

CHAPTER 9
The Great Quickening
◆

Some people have asked me in times past, "Dr. Halsey , why are you doing the things that you're doing ? " Well , let me tell you it was not my choice. Certainly , I was through a Seminary , but I was never a preacher , and I'm not a preacher now. This is not a church . It's a Brotherhood and there's a difference. I wanted an answer one time to a question on reincarnation . So I talked to the people of the churches and they would not even discuss it . Then I went to the theologians and they said, "That's one thing we don't talk about, headquarters wouldn't allow us to.

"I said, "If it's in the Bible it ought to be discussed . " There were nine of us student- ministers , so we got down and wrote on a piece of paper what we wanted to know. We wanted to know who Elijah was, if he was really John the Baptist like it says in the 11th chapter of Matthew.

You've read it. And we , in reading this section of the Bible decided we'd just write a note to Yahveh himself , and that two of us would get down and pray and the rest of us would pray that we would not waver in our prayers . And believe me, we had "fireworks " that night , and we got the answer. As a matter of fact , we were in a closed auditorium, all the windows were closed, or rather all the doors were closed. There were no windows.

And as we prayed , a wind began to blow from this "spiritual vortex" so hard that we could scarcely stand up because we could not stand the high vibrations. We thought we were going to be consumed right there.

Two weeks later, I'd gone to our home at Balboa, California, which was right on the beach. We had a place right on the jetty , and it was about 2:30 in the morning , and we'd been studying out some of these things that the churches would not talk about. We finally finished our talking and I was preparing for bed after that, when all at once I sensed that I was not alone. I was not by myself at all . But I did not see anyone, and it was a frightening experience , not being scared, but feeling that HIGH VIBRATION .

I didn't think that I could stand it. I knew I couldn't possibly stand it long . Here I'd been through a war and I was a grown man. Our older son and two of our girls were at home, and I went in and crawled into bed with my older son. I left the light .on -- I don't mind telling you -- and I knew it wouldn't do a bit of good. But I couldn't cope with this thing that I could not see. The vibrations were so terrific that I just could not stand it. I knew that I would surely die if it didn't let up.

After a few minutes, and in spite of this, I almost dozed off. And the Master came to me, and he spoke and everyone in this room could have heard it. It was not on the inside, it was on the outside where everyone could hear. And he said, "I have chosen you to teach the things that I will give you to teach, to those that I will send to you ! " So we don't go looking for people . You've never seen one of our advertisements any place . He said that he would send those whom he wanted to learn what he had to say.

This startled me so much that for about 10 or 15 minutes nearly 20 minutes that he talked to me - it startled me so much that I was busily contemplating the very first things that he told me, so that I can not tell you one thing he said in between. And I'd give almost anything to learn what he told me in that 15 minutes between the first part of the message -- if you want to call it that -- and the last of his visitation. But I do remember the last thing that he said: " If you will be faithful to carry out these commandments that I have given to you I will give you the desire of your heart. " Then I spent the next half hour to an hour trying to figure out what the desire of my heart was , because I DIDN'T KNOW!!!

He said, "As a sign to you, if you will pray for some one who is sick unto death I will heal them. " But we're told to "try the spirits " , isn't that true ? So we wanted to know that this thing was right . Now, my next door neighbor was a gentleman by the name of Hall , and he had been my neighbor previously when we had lived in Santa Ana. And I knew that Mr. Hall was in the hospital ready to die of thrombosis . He was an old man, and they had given him no hope. So I steamed by his house. I mean I really got in the car and went over there as quickly as I could and took two of the men with me who were present when we were asking for this heavenly information . I knocked at the door and Mrs Hall answered .

She said, " Shhhh! We just brought him home. They gave him no hope and we don't expect him to last the day . " I said, "I'd like to see him" , and she replied , " Shhhh! " I persisted , "I'd like to come in and see Mr. Hall. " "Well , come in , but you have to be quiet. Don't touch him, because any movement is going to cause him to go! "

ButI knew that the Master had spoken. So I went in and said, "Mr. Hall, you're going to be all right ! " His wife looked at me as if she just wanted to murder me, but I reached out and I took hold of his hand with both of mine, and two of our girls were at home, and I went in and crawled into bed with my older son. I left the light on -- I don't mind telling you -- and I knew it wouldn't do a bit of good. But I couldn't cope with this thing that I could not see. The vibrations were so terrific that I just could not stand it. I knew that I would surely die if it didn't let up.

After a few minutes, and in spite of this, I almost dozed off. And the Master came to me, and he spoke and everyone in this room could have heard it. It was not on the inside, it was on the outside where everyone could hear. And he said, "I have chosen you to teach the things that I will give you to teach, to those that I will send to you ! " So we don't go looking for people . You've never seen one of our advertisements any place . He said that he would send those whom he wanted to learn what he had to say.

This startled me so much that for about 10 or 15 minutes nearly 20 minutes that he talked to me - it startled me so much that I was busily contemplating the very first things that he told me, so that I can not tell you one thing he said in between. And I'd give almost anything to learn what he told me in that 15 minutes between the first part of the message -- if you want to call it that -- and the last of his visitation. But I do remember the last thing that he said: " If you will be faithful to carry out these commandments that I have given to you I will give you the desire of your heart. " Then I spent the next half hour to an hour trying to figure out what the desire of my heart was , because I DIDN'T KNOW!!! He said, "As a sign to you, if you will pray for some one who is sick unto death I will heal them. " But we're told to "try the spirits " , isn't that true ? So we wanted to know that this thing was right . Now, my next door neighbor was a gentleman by the name of Hall , and he had been my neighbor previously when we had lived in Santa Ana. And I knew that Mr. Hall was in the hospital ready to die of thrombosis . He was an old man, and they had given him no hope. So I steamed by his house. I mean I really got in the car and went over there as quickly as I could and took two of the men with me who were present when we were asking for this heavenly information . I knocked at the door and Mrs Hall answered .

She said, "Shhhh! We just brought him home. They gave him no hope and we don't expect him to last the day . " I said, "I'd like to see him" , and she replied , " Shhhh! " I persisted , "I'd like to come in and see Mr. Hall. " "Well , come in , but you have to be quiet. Don't touch him, because any movement is going to cause him to go! "

But I knew that the Master had spoken. So I went in and said, "Mr. Hall, you're going to be all right ! " His wife looked at me as if she just wanted to murder me, but I reached out and I took hold of his hand with both of mine, and said a prayer. I could feel electricity running out of my body, right up his arm. It was his left hand. And I said, "Mrs.Hall, he's going to be all right . " She looked at me as if she wanted to say, "You get out of here and never come back. Don't you have any respect for the dying ? "

So I excused myself , together with the other two gentlemen and we left. The next time I saw Mr. Hall was two months later , and when I passed by the old neighborhood he was pushing the lawn mower mowing his lawn. So I know that the Master told me right . That is the reason why I am standing here with you today , and I do it very humbly , because I feel that it is a responsibility to bring to you the things that you're hearing from out of this world, because they are in a great measure not of this world.

We're going to let you know a little bit more about what is taking place in the heavens insofar as the government there is concerned. There is not only the Melchizedek priesthood in the heavens and upon the surface of this world, which are designed to work hand in hand together for bringing all things into balance and placing this world back on course ; but you also have what are known as the Vorondadek Brothers, who are of a different order. They are more or less " record keepers " of everyone on the surface of this world . They have to record the whole business.

You will find that it says in the scriptures that Elijah is going to come again . And he's going to come for one thing , to turn the hearts of the children to their Fathers, and the hearts of the Fathers back to their children. Was it talking about your ancestors on this world ? Certainly not, because it is written, that you only have one Father which is the principal Father which is in heaven. But there are other fathers ofuniverses because they are the ones that are in charge of the creation of the universes . And these are the "fathers" that it is spoken of that Elijah is going to turn the hearts of the children back to, and the children of those universes back to the very builders of those universes. These fathers are known as "Constellation Fathers" . I hope that you have pencil and paper handy now because I'm going to give you some very significant information.

At least 3 Vorondadeks are assigned to the rulership of each of the 100 Constellations of what is called a "local universe" . Can you imagine a universe designated so, not by our scientists calculations, but by the calculations of our brothers and fathers upstairs ? Here are those calculations: One local universe is comprised of 100 -- by our count constellations . That is large , isn't it ? Isn't that tremendous ? We are told that in the 3rd density alone there are more than 40 billion suns and each of them has around it 12 ruling planets , and then 70 planets , and then many, many more planets which are subject to the 70. It is just like the organization that the Master had on this world, where he drew 12 around him in order to turn around and school the 70, and then the 70 were sent out as ministers unto all the rest. It is the same way in the heavenlies. These suns are selected by the Creator Sun and are commissioned by Gabriel as the most high of the constellations for service during one decamillennium, which is 10,000 of our standard years. That is a term of duty .

In their time it is 10,000 years precisely . But because we are placed farther out of the infinite light , and our vibrations are much slower here, there is a time- drag factor of about 5. For example , it takes us a long time here to say what we're going to say... like slowing down a phonograph record. You have a phonograph record that would normally play in 3 minutes, but you slow it down to where it has to take, maybe 15 minutes and you can hardly hear it talk. You know how it is.

Well, we are slowed down in our vibrations because we are out of true course, so our calculations would be about 50,000 years whereas their calculations would be 10,000 years of their standard time.

Now, the most high reigning Constellation Father has two associates -- a senior and a junior associate -- and with each change of administration the senior becomes the head of the government of all these 100 constellations of a local universe. The junior assumes the duty of a senior while the unassigned Vorondadek resident on the Salvington worlds which are in the central sun region of all of these 100 constellations , they nominate one of their number as candidate for selection to assume the responsibilities of junior associate. And each of the most high rulers , in accordance with the present policy , has a period of service on the headquarters of a constellation for 3 decamillenniums, which in our time is 150,000 years.

That's a long time, isn't it. But in ETERNITY , how long is it ? We are told that our lifetime is but a vapor -- it is but a breath . We are told that of our time here, that a 1000 years is but a day to Yahveh, where He is .

Someday I'm going to bring a tape here and play it for you. It is a taperecording of birds. You say, well, I've heard losts of birds. Well, I don't believe that you've ever heard a tape like this. There was a gentleman who went into the woods and he took a tape- recorder , and he taped the sound of birds singing , all of them. He even had some fishhawks and crows and all kinds of birds . Play the tape and you would say, that's the most jumbled- up mess I ever heard . But remember -- their vibrations are higher -- and what they say that quick can be spread out in our calculation of vibration for a long period of time. So he began to slow the music of all these birds down. He would record, and then he would slow it down and re- record it at a slower speed, and slow it down, until it had been slowed down eight times. Then he began to play the tape that he had recorded of the birds at this speed.

And it sounded like beautiful violins coming in from some symphony orchestra. And here is this old fishhawk that had such an angry sound, and such a bass voice that you could say, "Well , who would want to listen to that ?" Well, guess what ? He sings a song all the way through. And here is a crow that comes in and he sounds in on chorus with the old fishhawk singing tenor . Then you hear some other birds in the background as they join in on the chorus -- up and down like a beautiful chorus of voices --and you say, "That's not birds, that's heavenly music! " And that's exactly what it is , because music is a language of heaven, and every creation under the sun is going to one day understand the same song and the same music of vibration. This is part of our higher destiny .

I know where this tape is, and I can get it and play it for you. It is beautiful! We played it at our home on the desert for about a three week period . We just put it on the machine and played it, and guess what ? My wife began to play the songs on the organ . The children -- instead of singing commercials like they would pick up on the radio -- began to sing these bird songs. At school they would whistle them and the teacher would say, "Where in the world did you find a beautiful song like that ?" The children said , "Oh, we got it from a bird! " The teachers listened and said, "My , this is certainly unusual. " But this is a reality .

And one day soon we'll have this tape here for you to listen to. But what I'm trying to get across is that the vibration on all different levels , even the next vibration above us -- which is the bird level -- is much faster now. And we are told that every one of us is going to have to be QUICKENED in our mortal flesh, before we come into that consciousness and understanding where we will know what ALL THINGS are. Didn't the Master say that "I will QUICKEN you in your mortal flesh" ? That means he is going to increase your vibratory rate so that you can catch up with the song, because it's all dragged out where you are. You're not being given the whole picture because you can't receive it fast enough , and the things that you need to know cannot even be received in the span of a lifetime because the power fails before the record finishes playing , don't you see?

But the time is coming when you are going to be quickened , and you're going to get this whole story , and then you will understand what happened to the Master in his tomb, at the day of the resurrection. When they came and looked and they saw a stack of graveclothes , but the tomb was empty on the inside, they said, "How in the world did he get out of there?"

Well , from these very records we know that he was taken through a process of accelerated time -- which is a QUICKENING -- causing it not to string out in our vibration. But when they put the beam on him, it had brought the resurrection about that quickly ! And in the form that he is now in, he is known as the king which is invisible, immortal, eternal -- where? -- in the heavens, which is anywhere from the bottom of your feet upward. That's first Timothy 1:7 if you want to look it up.

These constellation fathers are very important to us. They are import-ant because they are a part of the heavenly government, and one day the kingdom government on the surface of this world is going to be a part of them. You say, "Well, I don't see them. Why don't they come down here?"

We are told that the things that are seen are temporary, and the things that are not seen are eternal. They are living on an eternal vibration and plane. You take an electric fan, and you say, "I can count four blades on that fan. So you plug it in and it begins to turn at 1725 RPM and you say, "I know there are 4 blades there. I can feel the breeze and I can't count the blades but I know that they're there. I can see them moving."

So you increase the speed up to 3400 RPM and you say, "I don't see any blades there," -- Don't stick your finger in it! If you do you're going to lose the finger. The 4 blades of the fan are there, but they have been quickened out of the vision of your mortal eyes. And there are many things around you that are absolutely real that are here to minister to you, to teach you and to help you that are far more real than YOU are on the out-side. They are like the inner man who has a body eternal in the heavens, that was not made by hands. That is the Melchizedek Elohim within you.

You will find that the Master pays visits to many of you. And you say, "Oh, I feel just like I am going to be carried away and I feel like I had a visitation!" Chances are you did." Well, why didn't I see him?" You were not QUICKENED to the place where you could see him, but you could feel his holy presence. He comes and goes, and he says, "If you can keep my commandments, you'll be loved of me. And if you're loved of me, you'll be loved of my Father whose name is Yahveh. And we will come to you and manifest ourselves to you and make our abode with you." John 14:21.

The "greater works" means to RE-move this world -- this "garden" that was planted -- and re-establish it back ON COURSE with infinite light. But in order to see that this comes about, we must have understanding from HIGHER AUTHORITIES -- way higher authorities than we are -- to bring the knowledge from where it was recorded, and bring it unto us even as TEACHERS. There are many people in this local universe whose intelli-gence is below ours, and believe me I feel sorry for them.

We are told that in the system behind us, of the sun behind us which our scientists call Rohr (it can be seen in the southern declinations below the equator) that there is not only one garden planet, but that there are 2 garden planets there. Why? Because the Luciferian forces inter-traveling from one system to another have caused this same trouble and chaos there.

For this reason, and for the widespread violence of the heavens, you are able to see stars and constellations. Haven't you watched the stars at night? Well, you saw them. And the very fact that you saw them indicates that they are in a temporary position, because it is written that things which are seen are TEMPORARY, but things which are not seen are ETER-NAL. For those planets of our system that are NOT out of course with the infinite light, but are beyond the realm of this imbalance, they are invisible as they are eternal. 800,000 of them are known as the reserve corps, and they have been brought now into this system.

All of these 100 constellations have Teachers and it is written in Isaiah, the 30th chapter, beginning with the 20th verse, that your Teachers will no longer be hid around the corner when you begin to drink the water of adver-sity and taste of the bread of affliction. But -- it says that when this time comes that your eyes are going to SEE your Teacher, not because they're going to come down to your level, NO. Right now you could not see them.

But it is written, that in this time when knowledge and wisdom shall be INCREASED in the world, that "I WILL QUICKEN YOU in your mortal body," said the Master, "and raise your vibration up to where -- there they are!" And you will converse back and forth. And as planetary princes you'll be working shoulder to shoulder to do the greater works: to set this whole sys-tem and systems and constellations of this local universe, back on course with infinite LIGHT, to cure the DISEASE in this "body" of Christ Consciousness which is everything that you see.

Now I want to tell you that the UFO beings and these higher Teachers I have been speaking about, constantly refer to a condition they call the "Frequency Barrier".[9] We are "below" this barrier and they are "above" it, in the sense that their vibrational frequency is much higher than ours, and so their mind normally functions in a cosmically "open" state, whereas ours is practically a "closed" state. This Frequency Barrier is more of a gate than it is a solid wall, and that gate can be opened. When Maldek was destroyed, causing our planetary system to be thrown violently off course, the Barrier was one result of the greatly lowered frequency of vibrations.

But listen! The Frequency Barrier is lifting. It has been steadily lift-ing since the year 1958 (when the sun completely reversed its polarity) And believe me, the brothers upstairs have not been idle in working to get this garden planet of ours back on course with infinite light. The "Great Quickening" is underway (proof of it is easily seen in the vast numbers of people now having visions, psychic powers, etc.) and you will feel it.

---

9. The term, Frequency Barrier was first used by W. Bateman

CHAPTER 10
The RE-Moval of Shan
◆

There is only one time when one planet can take the position of another planet and can be completely RE-moved and placed ON COURSE with this infinite light. That time comes once each 312,000 years when we change from one density to another. Remember, we are now in an anti-clockwise density which is negative. But we're rising all the time. And the 4th den-sity we are coming into is a positive polarity density whose vortice is in a clockwise motion. (refer to Chart #3 , page 12).

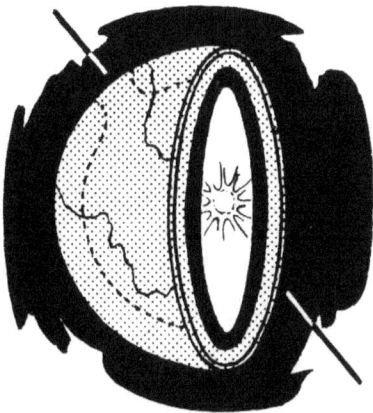

As we rise -- and we're in this arc of the overlap of these two densities right now -- it is a very important place, be-cause halfway through this arc will be the highest point to which we're been able to rise through this 3rd density at all. That is a very important place for us. It is a very important place because that is what is known as COSMIC HIGH NOON.

When we come to the exact center, right here between the arc, we will be equally in the force of the 4th density and the 3rd density. We passed into this arc on August 20, 1953. As we have worked up higher in this arc, intelligence has been increased. And there is a definite reason why it has increased.

True, people were intelligent 50 years ago. A lot of us have mothers and fathers and grandparents who were here more than 50 or 60 years ago. How many of you have someone living who is older than that? Don't you think that they're intelligent people? Certainly they are intelligent.

But they didn't have television, they didn't have telephones, they didn't have automobiles, they didn't have a whole lot of things that we have now. Why? Because we have been quickened. Our frequency has been increased as we have come closer to the 4th density, and more things have been open-ed up to us as far as intelligence is concerned. When we come fully into the 4th density it will not even be necessary for you to use voice for communication, because you'll be tuned into a plane where everyone will be on a thought level. Voice is a low frequency thought level. We have to think of something before we say it. If we were fully telepathic and someone in here would have a thought that they were going to go out and rob a bank, what would happen? Everyone would turn around and look at him, and say, "Look fella, you get up and fly right!"

That's the reason why we don't have a police department on many of the planets of this system that are closer in to this substance of faith than we are. Yet they're looking for something that is higher also. Don't kid your-self, they are out of course also, though not to the degree that we are. But when we all come into a position of BALANCE it's going to be wonderful. You'll know every thought, you'll be seen as you are seeing, you'll know as you are known, and that's what you are coming into. All intelligence will be on the same high level, and that will be with the Father.

So there won't be any intention of crime, or anything like that. It's all going to be happiness, and the vibration of love. When we come fully, and we're about 1/4 of a minute to the highest point in this 3rd density now, when we come right to the center of this arc -- then you're going to be able to start to see things around you that you didn't know were there. And the old bright sun that you see with your physical vision up here is going to start to fade, it's going to start to darken. So that those who have not yet built a spiritual consciousness which is a LIGHT WITHIN, will be troubled for the "night cometh when no man can work." Isn't that what it says?

As you pass over, the physical light of our sun is going to dim out to the natural man. The spiritual man on the inside is going to become that light. Those individuals shall be the light of the world at that time. Our brothers upstairs say, the spiritual people will be literal lights and they will be seen as lights out of darkness. This is because the sun, as "seed", has been planted into them. They are the "sun" of man, do you see? This is important for you to know, for certainly the END-TIME is deepening.

We'll come over to a position just beyond that, and this old world is go-ing to have a hard time finding its new poles. It's going to rock just like it was a cradle, and things are really going to be rough because it will be bucking two different vortices equally -- one positive and one negative in a position of motion in which one is completely contrary to the other.

When it comes over to this position, that quick , it will find its poles and it will take just a thousand years -- a millennium -- around this first turn, and then it will come just for a short season into the influence of a lower position in the arc of cosmo. I mean the overlap is a shorter distance on the next turn around of this 4th density, and just for a short season they will have a vivid remembrance of the old 3rd density. Then they'll pass out of it, and all of these things that you remember of sorrow and unhappiness will be gone forever, and I'm glad. But that isn't all of the important things we have to tell you about the cosmic re-establish ment of Shan (the cosmic name for planet earth). However, a question and answer session might be the better way to bring out this information. So, if you'll ask the questions, we'll do our best to answer them for you.

Q. Would you explain a little more about the changing polarity of the sun? A. All right. The polarity of the sun has a direct relationship to the po-larity of the planets around the sun, for there are 12 planets around the central sun. This world is turning from West to East at 980 miles an hour at the equator. And we know that the sun, being of a positive polarity, is traveling from East to West -- just the opposite direction. We also know that this world is UPSIDE DOWN (or nearly so) because of a cataclys-mic event at the time of the Flood, at the time of Noah. qualify that.

In the 42nd chapter of Isaiah, it is speaking about the sun coming up in the WEST. It says, "In the sun rising, and in the West.", because before the flood the sun DID come up in the West. And the very fact that it comes up in the East now is because we are UPSIDE DOWN.

The reversing polarity of one body naturally has an effect on other bod-ies and the fact that we are coming into the full influence of the 4th density is not only effecting the change in polarity of the suns of the different solar systems, but it is also effecting a change in the polarity of the worlds. The sun as it stands now is subject to the counter-clockwise vortice motion of the 3rd density. Naturally, the light forces that are coming through the 4th density have an opposite polarity. And, as we are coming to the center of the arc of cosmo, we have come to a place nearly of balance between the two vortices here. One being subject to an anti-clockwise polarity and one being subject to a clockwise polarity. As we are coming right up onto the change it is only natural that the source of infinite light be changed from that which is controlling the 3rd density to that which is controlling the 4th which has an OPPOSITE direction, causing our SUN to change its polarity.

Q. How much are we off course now, from the infinite light source?

A. The understanding that we have now is, that according to the position that we're now in, we're about 90 degrees instead of 180, out from the infinite light source, as far as being "upside down" is concerned.

Q. What is causing the great buildup of snow and ice-packs at the South Pole region, and could this ice-mass, 2 miles high, "flip" the world?

A. The RE-moval of this world is supposed to be a gradual proposition, not a violent thing. However, our nuclear scientists have done a lot of atomic bomb testing, which hasn't helped matters. They have, in fact, accelerated the tremendously massive weight buildup at the South Pole . At each bomb explosion , the radioactive particles go up into the ionisphere , and collect a certain amount of soil and water in our atmosphere that is definitely POSITIVE in polarity . It's immediately attracted to our negative polarity north pole. That causes the ice to melt, which rises in the form of vapor. It is immediately attracted, because it's negative, to our positive polarity south pole. But it doesn't get there. At about 70 degrees latitude south it begins to freeze and form a blob on the side of the world , and it tries to help the world to turn which causes it to TILT . We're told that if something like an atomic war would happen, this accumulation would be terrific , and we would flip as many as three times. Over and over and over.

Don't think IGY doesn't know about this , because they do. We've even had letters from them. If we leave this thing alone, it will tip easy and it will be a gradual proposition , according to the brothers upstairs .

Q. I would like to know if you have information on how far it is from the edge of the crust of the earth to the crust of the INNER EARTH ?

A. Yes, I can give you that information. The original shell of the earth is approximately 800 miles thick. It is of TRANSLUCENT substance. It will emit light . And when the crust of the world that does not belong here at all is flung off of this place, the inner sun's light will shine through . As regards the crust, it was gathered here . It's part of the great planet Maldek- Lucifer , the planet that was "cast out into all the earth" . And according to the IGY scientists in a report to Look Magazine , the July 8th edition, 1958 , it states that this fallout from this Luciferian source is still coming in at the rate of 3000 tons a day , upon the surface of this world.

After this debris- crust is flung off, then the light of the inner sun will begin to emit through the original shell of the earth, and then there will always be light on the surface of this world like it was in the beginning . There won't be any darkness at all , because you will be taking your light from the sun in the center of this world and the ocean that you have here which is a POSITIVE element. We have 3 positive elements on the surface of the world . One is salt, one is gold and one is silver. In each minute stage the positive elements are in a cube and we find this is true of the salt in ocean water . The salt waters came from the vaporous canopy that was at one time around the surface of the world, similar to the way Venus is now.

You will find that during the time of the flood, salt water rained down upon the surface of the world. That's the reason you have 2 kinds of water on this world, salt water and fresh water, and they're distinctly different. You will find that they do not even mix well . You can go out into the Gulf, and you will find fresh water out in the Gulf and you will also find salt water right next to it. So it doesn't mix up too well , because they are two different elements and magnetically they are alien. You'll find that it also tells you in the Bible that when this " Lucifer " will be cast into the bottomless pit, this Luciferian substance which is the crust of this world, will be magnetically flung into endless space.

The outer crust sits on top of the original shell of the world, and latest findings by IGY scientists show that this crust is approximately 250 miles thick. The thickness of this crust varies in different places . In the Mediterranean it is very shallow, very shallow. In other places , it is very thick. This world is PEAR - SHAPED. And the time will come when our sun that you see now will not be visible to our eyes at all . It will then be 7 times brighter than it now is , 7 times brighter . It tells you that in the 30th chapter of Isaiah . We are only partaking of about one- seventh the amount of light that normally we would have.

Q. Is our world going to remain pear- shaped during this coming change ?

A. No, it's shape will be corrected. The proton in the center of the world takes its energy from our present sun. When the present sun increases its energy by coming into balance with infinite light , coming into the center of this infinite light source, it will be multiplied by seven. The pressure in the INTERIOR of the world will then become 7 times greater than it is now. At that time this world will not be pear-shaped nor egg- shaped , but because of the pressure it will be brought back to its original SPHERE . It'll be blown-up as it were, by pressure just like a balloon. And that is the main thing that is going to crack all of the crust loose from this world.

If you want to explore this idea further , get a copy of the July issue of the Saturday Evening Post, for 1959. It has an article by a Harvard scientist named Charles

Hapgood, and it's titled: "The Earth's Shifting Crust". It's beginning to break up now. It's interesting to note that scientists have finally come out and drawn a picture showing that there is a great barrier at the south pole . Remember we talked about this two years ago? Well , they brought this idea out... it's supposed to be TOP- SECRET . But they brought it out just the same, showing that there is a great barrier where the ocean literally rises like a hill at the South Pole. It shows that there is a sun in the interior of the earth, and it shows that there is a space around the sun. It shows the CRUST of the earth and it shows another shell underneath the " shifting crust" . And it starts the article by the Harvard professor, Charles Hapgood, by stating that " science may be about to REWRITE the story of the earth". They're catching on!

They do not dare bring out all of the information that they have and know to be a fact, because it would cause the classroom books of all your universities to be obsolete . And they don't believe that the people are ready to believe the new information that would have to take its place !

Q. The 4th density doesn't necessarily mean a perfect situation, does it ?

A. Our commandment is to be perfect even as he is perfect . And so far as our minds are able to comprehend, we shall, in the 4th density, be of a much higher spiritual status, because nothing that is not spiritually quickened will be allowed to cross the Frequency Barrier into the 4th density . It will be a very big step toward that perfect situation you desire.

Q. When you were talking about going from the 3rd to the 4th density , were you referring to just our planet or did you mean our solar system ?

A. The whole system. Not only this system, but the system behind it. The system ahead of us has already transversed and gone over into the fourth density . Our sun, being ahead of us, has already changed its magnetic polarity , according to a scientific item that appeared in the Los Angeles Times , on Sunday , Oct. 25, 1959. It is already beginning to take its source of energy, not from the light that feeds the 3rd density , but from the light that feeds the 4th. And as we follow and come into that influence at Cosmic High Noon, then we are also going to change our polarity , and we're going to turn right - side up. We're going to turn right - side up.

Q. Are Venus , Mars and Earth operating in the 3rd Density now?

A. That's correct. They are.

Q. Are the other planets in our solar system which are visible to us, also operating in the 3rd density ?

A. In this system, all planets that are operating in the plane of the 3rd density , are visible to us because they are in a temporary position also, just as we are. You'll find that the life range is from 300 years upward on the planets in our system, and they're looking forward to an eternal situation just exactly like we are.

Q. What does our world look like , underneath its outer crust ?

A. This world is beautiful underneath the crust of this planet , according to the Bible and according to our friends upstairs . It says that a Kingdom lies buried in all of its glory and all of its riches. It has taken millions of years to be covered up by all of this fallout from Maldek, but one day soon when the fallout shakes loose, we'll see a beautiful, beautiful world.

CHAPTER 11
Ye Shall be Lifted Up
◆

Those people who build the proper force about them, when the brothers upstairs put a TRANSITOR BEAM from the craft, down upon them, it will defy the force of gravity and cause them to be weightless . They will then be taken right up on the transitor beam, into the craft . This is the kind of beam that George Van Tassel of Giant Rock, was taken up on, and also various other people . I believe it is the same type of energy beam that took Jesus up when he was raised up into the heavenlies. It says he was caught up into a CLOUD. He was taken up.

Many times these flying saucers, being positive in polarity , gather a vaporous canopy of moisture to themselves and appear as a cloud. I'm sure most all of you have seen pictures of UFO's and in most instances they have collected this moisture to themselves to where they look like a cloud. "When you see the sign of the Son of Man coming in the CLOUDS "

Clouds is plural . That means more than one. The Son of Man is he that planted the good seed. That seed isn't any particular one, it could be ALL of you here. I believe that it is . And you'll find that the boys upstairs have planted that seed pretty good, and now they are here in the clouds. "When you see the sign of the Son of Man coming in the clouds of glory , look up because your redemption draweth nigh . "

You say, "Sounds wonderful, Dr. Halsey , but I just don't see how it is possible to overcome gravity that easily , it is such a strong attractive force. How can this gravitational force be nullified like you say?"

Let me tell you some secrets relating to gravity . Gravity is not attractive. It is not attractive. You will find that the magnetic lines which you have always been taught is a "pole" that runs through the center of the world, is not a pole at all , but a combination of pressures that focus within the shell of the earth. These pressures consist of the pressure of the greater sun up here pushing down, and the pressure of the tiny inner sun in the earth pushing back. Those two forces each offer a steady pressure, one greater than the other, and these pressures are known as GRAVITY .

Another secret I want you to know about is that you have two vortices affecting you every day of your life . One vortex begins at the bottom of your feet and pulls down on your physical body. That vortex is caused by a terrific pressure, and is called gravity . It pulls you downward.

There is another vortex that begins at the top of your head and lifts up. It lifts up on the INNER man of you, or the SOUL man of you and this second vortex is called faith. You have been given a MEASURE of FAITH . The upper vortex has to equal the one that will pull you down, in order for you to be put into BALANCE spiritually as well as physically .

We've been told that you're going to be taken off the surface of this planet for the CLEANSING of this world when all the debris flys off and goes into endless space. What do you have to do now to prepare for this ? If you wake up some morning and turn around and say, "I wonder who I can take today ? I'll get to the top no matter who I step on! " , that is one thing I guarantee will UN-balance you on the negative side.

If when you get up in the morning you say, "What can I do to help someone today ? How can I plan my day to where this will be a better world because I live here? If I know someone over here, no matter whether I like them or not, if they need a word in season from me, how can I best share my light and understanding with them ?" If you will take this attitude, you will increase the upper vortex, and bring yourself into soul-balance.

And if you're anywhere near that balance, you can ride the transitor beam. If the balance is off to the negative side, pulling you down, they can turn that beam on you but you'll stay right here. If anything , it will repel you, to stay on the surface of this world. And in that case, when the time comes when this world is righted , and the debris- crust goes into the bottomless pit which is endless space, if you're standing on it I'm sure you're going to take a long ride. It will be a long , long ride. I mean that this is the way the debris will be literally flung off, or cast off from the surface of this world. And certainly you don't want to be cast off with it.

Now this solar system of ours is in the 3rd density . We call it "Contri" . It's getting ready to move fully into the 4th density which is "Blaau" . Right between the two densities is what is known as the arc of cosmo. I'm going to give you a view looking down on these two densities . Actually there are twelve densities around a central sun, which is only one of twelve more densities around a greater sun. And it goes and enlarges onward throughout infinity . No one, in the physical body, I don't suppose, has any real comprehension of how great this thing is . Looking down on these densities , we are reminded of our expanding universe, which is expanding, for as we have been rising in this 3rd density , we've been going around and around for a long period of time. We've been traveling around and around and around , going through this density at 11,000 miles a second. We've been penetrating it at 11,000 miles a second, but it takes a solar system about 312,000 years to go through one density. That's a long time.

I've mentioned these things to help clarify your thinking in regard to what has been happening, cosmically , within our local universe in the past as well as in the present moment. These are important things to know about, because they have a very important bearing on what is to take place in the immediate future. After we have successfully made the transit through the 3rd density into the full influence of the 4th, you'll find that there'll be three classes of people . What are these three classes ?

We're a three-fold being . We have a body, a soul and a spirit . We can take whichever course we want. We can take the natural man of flesh , and we can retain that natural body too . We can hang onto the soul which isn't the highest , or we can follow the spiritual essence. After the Frequency Barrier is lifted, and the planets are back on course with infinite light , the condition of life on earth will have been dramatically "up- dated" . We will be able to visit one planet to the other, because the morning stars will be able to sing together as they did once eons of time ago. We'll have communication, fluently and perfectly .

We'll be able to cover all the universe in harmony , and it's going to be wonderful. When you look at the stars , and you look at the moon and look at the sun, they're not of the same BRIGHTNESS are they ? All right . That's how it will be with all of us. If we have the Christ light within, radiating strongly right now, after this planet has been placed back on course with infinite light , we will have the brightness of the sun in comparison with the stars and the moon. I mean we'll actually be seen as light . Light has different degrees of brightness .

The Master gave us quite an example of this , when he was taken into a high mountain apart , he was transfigured before them and his face shone as the SUN, and his raiment was white as the LIGHT .

A friend of ours and a friend of Mr. George Van Tassel as a matter of fact it was two friends , two ladies and their father and husband respectively -- were going through the desert. They were facing the sun and they stopped, and they got out of their car and they were kicking around in the desert and the sun was just on the horizon in the East . It was blinding them and they couldn't see where they were going. They decided it was a little too chilly , so they turned back toward their station wagon into the sun and they noticed that two gentlemen were walking up behind the station wagon. They looked and said they never saw anything quite like these people. They spoke , and the gentlemen spoke and went over a knoll on the hill .

In about 5 minutes they saw a large , shiny object -- it looked almost like a transparent pearl -- it was a flying saucer, about 150 feet in diameter. Then it took off.

The mother said to the daughter , "I wasn't going to say anything but did you see anything unusual about those people we just met? " "I sure did, mother. " "What did you see ?" "When I looked at them in the sun I could see the car right through them! "

They were the Sons of Adonai. They're in a frequency higher than we are. Their face shone as the sun, and their raiment is as white as the very light . And it tells you clearly , in the 13th chapter of Isaiah, that he's going to have people, like the gold of Ophir , which was transparent to the physical eyes. But it is these higher frequency beings who have been designated by the All - Father, to assist in the raising of those of us will be lifted up.

If you want to hear a prophecy concerning those who shall be lifted , a very good one is given in the Apocalypse of Thomas . You won't find that book included in your present version of the Bible, because it happens to have been excluded (along with several other very informative books such as the Book of Enoch, the Book of Jasher , etc.) by the Church fathers. Few people even know of or have even heard of this prophecy , but here it is :

"Then shall their bodies be CHANGED into the image and likeness and the honour of the holy angels and into the power and image of mine holy Father. Then shall they be clothed with the vesture of life eternal, OUT OF THE CLOUD OF LIGHT which hath never been seen in this world. For that cloud cometh down out of the highest realm of the heaven from the power of my Father. And that CLOUD shall compass about with the beauty thereof all the spirits that have believed in Me.

Then shall they be clothed and shall be borne by the hands of the holy angels like as I have told you aforetime. Then also SHALL THEY BE LIFTED UP into the air upon a CLOUD OF LIGHT (a spacecraft) and shall go with me rejoicing into heaven. They shall continue in the light and honour of my Father and there shall be unto them great gladness with my Father and before the holy angels "!

Now I'd like to tell you the story of little Johnny , and how he learned to overcome the vortex of gravity , so he could be LIFTED UP. I believe that there is something of value in this story, for all of us.

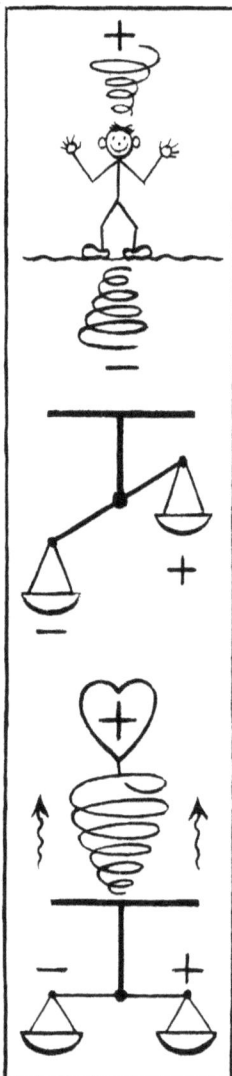

From the time Johnny was born, he was told how to prepare to die. Day by day the vortex called gravity pulled him down deeper and deeper . This vortex would have pulled him into a grave eventually . He was held in bondage to it. To him this drawing force became fear , so we will call it Fear. For years Johnny walked through the valley of life in the shadow of FEAR . He had been taught that he should be perfect . He even tried to become the stature of a perfect man. However , day by day he waxed older , more tired , and more confused. One day Johnny decided that he did not have all the Truth because he was in bondage to something that was causing him to grow old. He had heard that prayer changes things , but that only Truth can make one free. So Johnny started a search for Light , and this is what he found. After a good deal of searching , he learned that before you can come to the stature of a perfect man, you must first come to the knowledge .

Right away this realization gave Johnny a new lease on life , and this is the knowledge that he received. First of all , he learned that two UNSEEN FORCES have a direct bearing on all that he is . For instance, this vortex called gravity begins at his feet and pulls downward on his PHYSICAL body . He learned also that there is another force beginning at the top of his head and upward that endeavors to raise the INNER body or SOUL.

Now this upper vortex is vitally important , but how on earth does it work ? Also , how does he know where he stands in his present condition? It was explained to him like this: FAITH is the substance of things hoped for , the evidence of things not seen. The Christ within you is the hope of glory . Faith is the very substance of this Christ . And so that Johnny can have the knowledge of where he now stands, he was told that everyone is given a MEASURE of FAITH . So Johnny must USE that measure.

He does, and this is what he finds . He finds that FEAR tips the scales. This fear is pulling his physical body way out of balance with his spiritual body. (soul). So Johnny asked, "How can I balance the scales ?"

Right away, he was answered like this: "Johnny , when your soul is filled with the love of God, and your heart is sending love and light , or when you respond to the beautiAlle ful chords of the music of your soul, then you feel light on your feet. You feel LIFTED UP and enjoy a trembling sensation. Lifting you is the vortex of LOVE and we will call it trembling . Now remember this vortex called trembling is very much a part of your measure of faith. With this measure of faith you must WORK out your salvation with FEAR and TREMBLING . When you come to the unity of + FAITH , the scales will be balanced for true FAITH will at once render FEAR null and void .

When the scale is balanced you have come to the measure of the stature. You have come to the unity of the FAITH . You are set free by the power of TRUTH. Now Johnny , this is how it is accomplished . First of all we will make a partial list of the things that will increase fear! -- - : hate, selfishness, greed , jealousy , love of riches, temper , self-first others-last, adverse thoughts , over- eating, lies, cheating , closing mind to light , following precepts of man, etc.

"Now here are some of the things that will increase trembling : see God in everything , send love and light to all , rejoice and know that you are a part of creation, love thy neighbor as thyself , return good for evil , live the golden rule, look for kind things to do, live love, do not gossip , be like the Master Christ, keep a clean mind always."

Johnny is going to apply this to his daily life , and this is going to be a portion of his reward: He is going to have the mind of FAITH , unspeakable joy , health, youth eternal, love of God in his heart.

He will not be bound to this earth any longer , he will travel by the power of the spirit like Jesus did in Luke 4 and other places .

He will walk on the water. (gravity nullified).

He will hold the power of multiplication . And he will do the greater works, and

YOU CAN TOO, IF you will apply this New- Age truth.

This truth will set you FREE .

And truly HE, the Spirit of Truth, will take of things of the Lord and show them unto you. HE, the Spirit of Truth, will guide you into all Truth and show YOU things to come.

Now is the time that we should come to a place of conscious understanding and to the realization that only truth can make us free. Not doctrines, not ordinances, not creeds and not dogmas ... but truth (actuality) .

We are leaving the dark age of churchianity and entering into the New, Aquarian Age of Light , Truth and Christ Consciousness.

CHAPTER 12
The END-TIME Prophecy
◆

(SPECIAL NOTE : The reader is asked to please re-read the Introduction before reading this final chapter on the END-TIME Prophecy.)

The Spirit of Truth is come, hearken ye and heed these words . For I say unto you these things shall surely come to pass . Prepare thyself and seek wisdom. Look continually upon the things of God. A great work have I prepared for thee and a mighty work shall thou do. Thy name shall be known throughout the nation, and many shall call thee blessed of Me.

I am seeking to deliver My people from the hands of the enemy, and this have I called thee to do. My hand shall be upon all thy labors and My blessings shall rest upon all thy doings . Let thy faith soar mightily and trust in Me. This work is My work and I shall honor all of thy requests that are for this cause . Fear not to call upon Me for aid in all thou doest. My hand I have stretched forth and with a might higher arm I shall be with thee. Call unto My people, and gather them by the multitudes.

Speak unto them these things that I have shown unto thee that are soon coming to pass. Tell them the Great Beast is coming into the land to devour My people . He is the anti-Christ that shall seek to destroy all who cometh not after him. This man shall be mighty in deeds and wonders and his proclamations shall chill the hearts of men.

In My fierce anger have I allowed this thing to come upon the nation. These people have not sought after Me, nor called upon My name. They have gone their way and followed after their own imaginations . Mine anger has been kindled against this disobedience. Have I not said, "I am their God and they are My people ? Yet they follow after the gods of this world and they trust in their own strength . My word have they cast from them, and My name they have not honored. My cleansing they have not sought, nor My will nor way followed.

My Spirit has not ceased from dealing with their souls, yet they have no time to heed My voice.

I shall punish this nation for its untowardness and the ungodliness that fills the land. The time of My wrath and judgement has come, and who shall stand against Me? Like a whirlwind it shall sweep the nation, like a wild beast upon the prey shall this thing sweep forth, and in the fierceness of mine anger I shall consume the land. Desolation shall come upon it , and who shall comfort the desolate?

I have poured out My Love upon the world from the beginning , but their thanksgiving and praise have they withheld. They have not called upon My name nor sought My way. They have not considered in their heart, nor received My counsel. Let them now abide in their own strength and seek their own wisdom. Let them deliver themselves from the mouth of the devourer and the hand of the oppressor . Let their own feet carry them to refuge , but My refuge they shall not find.

In that day many shall come in My name saying , the Lord has sent me. These are Mine, and are sent of Me. They seek deliverance from the cold and hunger , and a refuge have I prepared for them.

I am raising up in the midst of thee a people who shall do My will in that day. I am beginning a PREPARATION throughout the land, and many are seeing the vision . Many others shall be added unto thee, and they shall go forth and teach the things that I have taught thee.

Let My people who are called by My name seek My face and know My will . Let their hearts be turned to Me and their prayers be heard throughout the land. I am preparing in their midst this work of mercy and deliverance and none shall suffer in the day of wrath IF My people obey My voice. If they obey not, suffering shall come upon many and many shall go into captivity because of the oppressor .

DELIVERANCE is for all My people, and great deliverance shall I prepare for them . In that day I shall raise up a great prophet. He shall declare My soon-coming with great power . My Spirit shall be mightily upon him and My words shall flow from his lips . This man shall prophesy in My name and tell thee of things soon to come to pass. He will be a great man of strength and signs and wonders shall follow his ministry .

Hear this man, and all he tells thee, and follow My instructions for he is of Me. He has a message for all to hear. His sayings are strange sayings , but they are Mine. You shall soon know him, and his presence shall be among you. All who hear this man and follow his instructions shall be delivered in that day .

107

I shall soon send My Spirit into the midst of My people and great rejoicing shall be throughout the land. Their joy shall be increased and their love enlarged and their hearts shall be turned unto Me. And their prayers with weeping, I shall hear again . This is the time of My visitation among My people , when I shall visit them and draw them together .

My Spirit shall come into their midst without measure, and a great knitting - together of My people shall take place . None shall say that anything is his, but shall sell all and follow Me. The days upon the earth are numbered, and the length thereof is short. Let no man gather together 9 into himself and say he is of Me. My Spirit shall bear witness with My word. If any man does draw away into himself and heedeth not My instruction he shall fall into the hands of the enemy and be numbered among the poor and the oppressed .

The cattle upon a thousand hills are Mine, and the world and all that is contained therein. I am gathering together My own in these last days , and in groups they shall assemble. They shall sell all and go into the mountains. They shall dig them out habitations and fortify themselves against that day . Let My word dwell in you and take root that you might know My voice and seek My will . I will reveal it unto you if you seek Me diligently.

Call a fasting and a prayer season, and wait upon Me until I reveal all unto thee. I am willing to give thee light if thou seekest and willing to answer thy prayers if thou shalt call upon Me. I am not slothful toward thee, nor do I withhold knowledge from thee.

Seek knowledge and it shall be given . Seek wisdom and it shall be granted without measure. I am doing a last days work and My people must seek My will and know it. It draweth nigh - the day draweth nigh . My coming is soon and My promises are sure. I have waited long and borne with man, but the end has come. A few more seasons and all shall be finished, and My work upon the earth completed .

I shall gather My people from the four corners of the earth, comfort the afflicted and seek the lost, strengthen the weak and pray for their infirmities . Call a solemn fast in thine assemblies and pray for My will in this work I am beginning to do in thy midst. I will answer and instruct thee, and thou shalt know My voice.

Care for the widows and their children, my son, in that day . My poor are precious unto Me. Leave them not behind and they shall be a help unto thee. BEGIN THY

PREPARATION SOON. Lay the groundwork and prepare the bins. Begin storing away, and forget not thy fuel, for it shall be gathered in that day . Bury it in pits underground , coal and wood shalt thou burn in that day , and I shall consume the smoke and hide it from the eyes of the enemy. I shall make air where there is no air in that day, and wisdom shall be given thee to prepare for ventilation .

All things must be hidden. They shall seek to search thee out, and shall not find thee if thou obeyest My voice . My mountains shall ring with thy shouts, and they shall not hear, and My heart shall be gladdened by thy praise . Thou shalt have peace like a river , and thy joy shall be in Me.

These warnings I must give thee. Prepare not for thyself alone, for many shall I send into thy midst. They shall come from afar, and shall come from near. Turn not away any, but prepare for many. It will be better to have a surplus than a lack in that day . If thou puttest all that thou hast into My work none shall lack . All that thou holdest back shall be lost. All that thou givest shall be returned.

Take heed unto the ants in the anthill . None has more than the others. None seekest honors nor heedest the doings of the others. All go about their own labors and toil from morning till evening , and harmony dwells among them. As thou dwellest in thy underground habitation, remember this little fellow that covers the universe. Consider his way. If one has a burden too heavy to bear, do not many come to help him ? One does not say, I will let the others lift the load while I watch and wait, but all go forth that are near, to struggle together till the load is lifted.

An ant is not selfish, but gives over to others.

An ant is not greedy , but seeks only the necessities.

A An ant is not gluttonous , nor followeth after feastings .

There is no wickedness in the way of the ant, but he labors on to do My will .

An ant is clean and polished , and his work neat. He cometh and goeth in haste to do My will , and none turneth him aside.

He argues not with his fellows, nor strives against them, but worketh in unison, that their work be accomplished.

So if this cometh from an ant, is this not wisdom? Work together , My people , and consider the ways of the ant. Go into the house of the Lord and seek My face until I reveal My will unto thee. Remain prayerfully before Me at all times and fast much before Me. My eye is upon thee and My ear attuned to thee, and in My love I am calling upon thee to do My will .

THESE are the things that I shall show thee that shall come to pass shortly upon the earth. It shall be in that day that I will raise up in the midst of thee a great prophet . He shall be likened unto the first prophet , and shall prophesy in My name things that shall shortly come to pass. He shall warn My people to flee from the wrath to come. Many shall hearken unto his voice and turn from their wicked ways, but many shall not hearken.

And great shall be the misery and distress that shall come upon them, for I shall have no pleasure in their ways.

In that day shall come forth a mighty voice crying unto My people to forsake their wickedness , and to follow in My way. These two prophets shall be mighty in works and deeds and shall turn many from their ways. My two prophets shall be mighty in the land, and their cry shall be heard to the ends of the earth. These two shall stand. They shall stand by Me even to the end of the earth, and great shall be their reward. I say these things unto thee and lie not, for My word endureth forever . It shall be in that day that I shall send My two prophets before the face of the people , and they shall declare My law unto them.

They shall cry out in righteousness and shall weep in mourning for My people . Their cries shall be heard to the ends of the earth, for this is My will . They shall declare the wrath of God against the enemy and all who call upon other gods . Their cries shall go forth and declare the righteousness of God before the people, and shall turn many from their ungodly ways.

These prophets are My anointed that shall stand before the throne of God, and they shall be faithful unto the end. These two shall not hearken unto the enemy, nor turn from My way, but shall do My will in all things . They shall stand in the last day before My Father, and I shall declare their righteousness unto Him. Great shall be their reward.

In that day I shall raise up a governor before the people, and he shall be cruel and have no mercy. His voice shall be terrible , and his sayings hard to bear. He shall come with a great army, and destroy like a swarm of locusts before a green field . Like the army of the damned, he shall eat of thy store, and many shall be left desolate. His mighty army shall slay the young men and rip open the woman with child . In their fierceness they shall slay the innocent, and rape and murder shall be their delight . Great fear and weeping shall cover the land, and sorrow shall be their portion. They have drunk of their cup of their fornication and lewdness and considered not My way. My wrath shall come upon them , and I will not consider their afflictions nor amend My way.

This is the reward I shall mete out to them in that day . I will send My army into their midst and destruction and sorrow shall come upon them . Let them not say, God is wicked. My people have done wickedly , and this is My righteous judgement against their wickedness . My people have not considered My way, but have followed after their own ways. Broad is the way that leadeth to destruction, but narrow and straight is My way that leadeth to everlasting life , and few do enter therein. I shall also send upon the land a great famine.

The people shall cry aloud for food and I will not hearken. They shall fall on the streets and call aloud to Me for food, but My ear shall be deaf. I will hearken unto My people who are called by My name, and shall deliver them from the enemy. But those who call not upon My name in the day that I dealt with them, I will not hear in the day that they call upon Me for deliverance from the enemy and famine.

Let there not be any that forsake My way in that day . Say not unto thyself, the hand of the Lord is too severe. The hand of the oppressor shall be more severe in the day of destruction. There shall be among My people at that time a common thing ; they shall hold fast to their gods of Vanity . This thing I detesteth ; it is a thorn in the flesh. Cast down thy idols and come before Me clean and bare. Let there be no uncleaness among you and let all flesh be crucified. As I died in the flesh for your sins, so die you out to all sins and let there be no filthiness among you.

In that day I shall raise up a standard in thy midst. I shall send forth an alarm throughout Zion, and a cry throughout the land. I shall call upon My people to assemble themselves together in My name and weep and mourn upon Mine altars . They shall cry out in the anguish of their soul and I shall hear them. My altars shall be wet with tears and my pews shall be empty in that day , for My warning shall go forth and many shall hearken. I shall raise up a standard among My people against the enemy and they shall know My will in that day . I shall put My will into their hearts, and they shall know the way I have prepared for their doings . If they have entered into My truth -- they shall know.

I will not reveal My will unto those who have refused My truth and have not entered therein, and this is My will . Great shall be the distress that shall befall the land in that day . Nation shall rise against nation, kingdom against kingdom . Great strife shall be throughout the land. Many shall raise and many shall fall ; many shall be brought low and many shall be exalted. All things must be done according to My will .

I know the way of the wicked and the way of the transgressor is hard ; let the wicked turn from his ways and the transgressor amend his ways. Let them cry aloud to Me and declare their ungodliness . I shall hear and cleanse them if they repent. If they love not Godliness, My arm shall not rest upon them, but My wrath shall come upon them and great destruction, great fear and terror shall be in their land in that day . He that feareth My wrath and turneth unto Me shall be saved, and he that feareth not My wrath shall know it -- for it shall be his portion .

Now there cometh upon the land a great earthquake , with great destruction. It shall destroy many people and much property. Great destruction shall be in it . Many shall be swallowed up in the earth, both great and small. It shall come upon all the land, and this shall tear down the strongholds of the enemy and send confusion. Great shall be the destruction; all hearts shall be faint and all hands shall be weak . There shall be none that shall stand against it, and all power shall fail . All shall be in derision, and every man shall flee to the mountains and cry out for the rocks to fall on them. They shall wander homeless, like beasts, in that day and each man shall be for himself. The strong shall slay the weak and eat his flesh and fathers shall eat their newborn babies before they cry.

I shall give them the heart of beasts, and they shall be as beasts. They honored not the God that created them and worshipped a BEAST that was no God. My people shall be LIFTED from the land before that day , for the end is near. Then cometh the destruction of all things.

My voice shall speak -- and all things shall be completed in that day . Then I , in My wrath, shall END the wickedness of this generation ; it shall know and see all these things come to pass. THIS IS MY WILL .

Hear this, all ye inhabitants of the land, great destruction cometh upon the earth and great destruction cometh. It shall come in thy time and among thy people . Proclaim this unto the land. Proclaim this unto the land. Let not thy feet be weary, nor thy heart afraid. Shout it unto the multitudes, proclaim it unto the masses, and let not thy voice be still -- for great destruction do cometh.

I am weary of their backslidings , weary of their evil ways, and tired of their pride and vanities. Their mouths speak great words, and proclaim great sayings , but their hearts are far from doing the things they speak . Their feet go about shedding blood, and the folly of their crookedness cometh up before Me. Shall I have pleasure in these things and forget their iniquities ? Shall their whoredoms and fornication go unpunished ?

I am a righteous God and My wrath is true, and My word is Truth. Surely , for their sins they shall be punished and My peace shall not rest upon their souls. He that dieth in his sins shall see death, and hell shall encompass him. But he that dieth with his sins forgiven , shall live in hope and die in peace. Mine he shall be in that day , and Mine throughout eternity for I am his God.

My soul shall have no pleasure in the sinful man in that day , for he seeketh not My great salvation and My blood is not upon his soul. Speak it unto the people of the things that I have told thee. I love these people but they love not Me. My heart is wrenched and torn at their backslidings and evil ways. They seek Me not, nor do they call upon My name, yet will I turn unto them if they turn unto Me and I will heal their backslidings and cure their ways if they come to Me and call upon My name.

They say unto themselves they have much, but they have nothing . They say they are rich, but they are poor. Their wealth is nothing, an abomination in My sight . Will I not punish a wicked people for their wickedness ? I shall send great destruction upon them in that day , and they shall speak evil of this way, but THEY are evil . By the hand of an evil oppressor they shall be led captive . Great slaughter shall be in their midst and great oppression . THEN shall they remember their evil and know that I am God.

Remind them of their evil in this day and they might repent and put away the evil from their midst. Say unto them, thus sayeth the Lord: If thou shalt repent of thy evil and put away thy backslidings I shall be thy God and thou shalt be My people . If thou repent not of thy evil , and put not away thy backslidings , I will come upon thee in that day and thou shalt taste of the plagues I shall put upon thee. And the end shall be utter destruction. I love the souls of My people, but My eyes gaze upon their wickedness. In that day I shall come upon the earth with a HEALING BALM, and heal all who call upon My name.

My Spirit shall rest upon them, and My love shall cover the earth. My voice shall shout from the mountaintops and be heard to the utmost part of the earth. Then shall the earth mourn and weep, lamentations shall be heard throughout the land and great weeping among the people . They shall be taken with great sorrow, for they know the Lord cometh and they are left desolate .

Weep not Zion, My people, for thou shalt be comforted. Lift up thy hands and rejoice for thy redemption draweth nigh . The night is over, a new day is dawning. THOU SHALT BE LIFTED UP FROM THIS OLD WORLD AND A NEW KINGDOM IS THINE .

The stars shall shine in His brightness and thy King shall reign forever. Great and abundant is the love of My Father and His wisdom exceeds that of all men. In His righteousness shall He reign , and His people shall rejoice in His greatness. His beauty shall exceed all the beauty of the earth and His love shall abound towards His people . Let none say He is unjust ; let all say He is RIGHTEOUS and judges in righteousness .

I have proclaimed a new day , I have begun a new work. The day of the end is at hand. Let all who dieth in righteousness be judged in righteousness, and all who dieth in unrighteousness reap an unrighteous man's reward. This is wisdom and justice , and let no man say he has been defrauded for righteousness has been his judge .

I have kept My word and My sayings are true. If a man regard not My sayings , that maketh Me not a liar nor an unrighteous judge , for My truth commandments are the law. If a man walketh not in them he is not of Me, but a servant of the masters he serveth.

If a man walketh in My statutes and My laws My love dwelleth in him, and he is mine. For by Me you knoweth the law. If you love Me you shall keep My commandments. I shall walk by thy side and guide thee if thou knowest My will and doeth it . I shall forsake none that walketh in Me; My love shall abide upon him as an everlasting shadow and My Spirit shall be his strength . His comings and his goings shall be guided by Me, and his thoughts shall be void of all evil .

Come together My people , assemble yourselves . Cry out aloud unto Me for deliverance from the hand of the enemy. Shout My praises and sing My songs and let thanksgiving and praise be in thy midst.

Did I not raise thee up from the dungeons ?

Did I not deliver thee and redeem thee from the curse of hell?

Are not My promises and My praises qualified , and am I not worthy of thy songs ?

I am thy God that created thee and thy God which sanctifieth thee. Am I not worthy of thy praise?

Cometh to Me with a great shout, for thine is the victory . Thou art the conqueror and the spoil is thine.

Take up the sword and the spear and go forth and My reward shall follow thee .

It will soon be past.

The END is near.

Thou shalt hear My voice as a trumpet sounding. Then shall the outcast mourn and weep, but THOU shalt be comforted, and THY JOY SHALL EXCEED ALL BLESSINGS

THE END